Widdings.

5/-

3/3.

THE HOME UNIVERSITY LIBRARY
OF MODERN KNOWLEDGE

204

THE INDUSTRIAL REVOLUTION

1760 – 1830

The
Industrial Revolution

1760 – 1830

T. S. ASHTON

*Professor of Economic History
in the University of London*

Geoffrey Cumberlege

OXFORD UNIVERSITY PRESS

LONDON   NEW YORK   TORONTO

1948

PREFACE

No one who teaches at the London School of Economics can ever be sure how much of what he writes is his own and how much belongs to his associates and pupils. This book is based on the work of many scholars (not all of whom will agree with the interpretation it offers). In particular, my colleagues H. L. Beales and F. J. Fisher have contributed perhaps more than they realize. The paragraphs on the cotton industry and on the standard of life of the workers are drawn from the researches of Miss Frances Collier of the University of Manchester, and those on the coal and iron industries have gained from the reading of an unpublished thesis by A. H. John. The statistical material, without which the book could hardly have been written, was assembled by a former student, W. Ashworth; and the final chapter owes something to brief conversations with Professor W. W. Rostow of Harvard. I thank them all.

LONDON   **T. S. A.**

May 1947

CONTENTS

PREFACE V

I INTRODUCTION I

II THE EARLIER FORMS OF INDUSTRY . . . 23

III THE TECHNICAL INNOVATIONS . . . 58

IV CAPITAL AND LABOUR 94

V 'INDIVIDUALISM' AND 'LAISSER-FAIRE' . . 127

VI THE COURSE OF ECONOMIC CHANGE . . 142

BIBLIOGRAPHY 162

INDEX 165

CHAPTER I

INTRODUCTION

IN the short span of years between the accession o
George III and that of his son, William IV, the face of
England changed. Areas that for centuries had been
cultivated as open fields, or had lain untended as common pasture, were hedged or fenced; hamlets grew into
populous towns; and chimney stacks rose to dwarf
the ancient spires. Highroads were made—straighter,
stronger, and wider than those evil communications that
had corrupted the good manners of travellers in the days
of Defoe. The North and Irish Seas, and the navigable
reaches of the Mersey, Ouse, Trent, Severn, Thames,
Forth, and Clyde were joined together by threads of
still water. In the North the first iron rails were laid
down for the new locomotives, and steam packets began
to ply on the estuaries and the narrow seas.

Parallel changes took place in the structure of society.
The number of people increased vastly, and the proportion of children and young people probably rose. The
growth of new communities shifted the balance of
population from the South and East to the North and
Midlands; enterprising Scots headed a procession the
end of which is not yet in sight; and a flood of unskilled,
but vigorous, Irish poured in, not without effect on the
health and ways of life of Englishmen. Men and women
born and bred on the countryside came to live crowded
together, earning their bread, no longer as families or
groups of neighbours, but as units in the labour force of

factories; work grew to be more specialized; new forms of skill were developed, and some old forms lost. Labour became more mobile, and higher standards of comfort were offered to those able and willing to move to centres of opportunity.

At the same time fresh sources of raw material were exploited, new markets were opened, and new methods of trade devised. Capital increased in volume and fluidity; the currency was set on a gold base; a banking system came into being. Many old privileges and monopolies were swept away, and legislative impediments to enterprise removed. The State came to play a less active, the individual and the voluntary association a more active, part in affairs. Ideas of innovation and progress undermined traditional sanctions: men began to look forward, rather than backward, and their thoughts as to the nature and purpose of social life were transformed.

Whether or not such a series of changes should be spoken of as 'The Industrial Revolution' might be debated at length. The changes were not merely 'industrial', but also social and intellectual. The word 'revolution' implies a suddenness of change that is not, in fact, characteristic of economic processes. The system of human relationships that is sometimes called capitalism had its origins long before 1760, and attained its full development long after 1830: there is a danger of overlooking the essential fact of continuity. But the phrase 'Industrial Revolution' has been used by a long line of historians and has become so firmly embedded in common speech that it would be pedantic to offer a substitute.

The outstanding feature of the social history of the

period—the thing that above all others distinguishes the age from its predecessors—is the rapid growth of population. Careful estimates, based on figures of burials and christenings, put the number of people in England and Wales at about five and a half millions in 1700, and six and a half millions in 1750: when the first census was taken in 1801 it was a round nine millions, and by 1831 had reached fourteen millions. In the second half of the eighteenth century population had thus increased by 40 per cent., and in the first three decades of the nineteenth century by more than 50 per cent. For Great Britain the figures are approximately eleven millions in 1801, and sixteen and a half millions in 1831.

The growth of population was not the result of any marked change in the birth rate. During the first four decades of the eighteenth century, it is true, the number of births per thousand people seems to have risen a little. Farm labourers tended to set up households of their own instead of boarding with their employers, and a decline of the system of apprenticeship in industry also led to earlier marriage and larger families. But from 1740 to 1830 the birth rate appears to have fluctuated only very slightly: for no decade does the estimate rise above 37·7, or fall below 36·6. Throughout the industrial revolution fertility was high but steady.

Nor can the increase of people be attributed to an influx from other countries. In every decade men and women took ship from Ireland to England and Scotland, and at times of dearth the trickle became a stream. But there was no such torrent of Irish immigration as was to come in the last five years of the eighteen-forties. On the other hand, during the eighteenth century perhaps a million people left Britain to seek a living overseas, mainly in the colonies. Among them were some 50,000 criminals transported to Maryland or Botany Bay, and a number of artisans who defied the law by carrying their technical knowledge and skill to Europe—not in the long run, it may be guessed, to the disadvantage of their native land. On balance, Britain was not a receiving centre but a breeding-ground for new communities across the seas.

It was a fall of mortality that led to the increase of numbers. In the first four decades of the eighteenth century excessive indulgence in cheap gin and intermittent periods of famine took a heavy toll of lives; but between 1740 and 1820 the death rate fell almost continuously—from an estimated 35·8 for the ten years ending in 1740 to one of 21·1 for those ending in 1821. Many influences were operating to reduce the incidence of death. The introduction of root crops made it possible to feed more cattle in the winter months, and so to supply fresh meat throughout the year. The substitution of wheat for inferior cereals, and an increased consumption of vegetables, strengthened resistance to disease. Higher standards of personal cleanliness, associated with more soap and cheaper cotton underwear, lessened the dangers of infection. The use of brick in place of timber in the walls and of slate or stone instead of thatch in the roofs of cottages reduced the number of pests; and the removal of many noxious processes of manufacture from the homes of the workers brought greater domestic comfort. The larger towns were paved, drained, and supplied with running water; knowledge of medicine and surgery developed; hospitals and dispensaries increased; and more attention was paid to such things as the disposal of refuse and the proper burial of the dead.

Since there are no reliable statistics it is not possible to say which age groups of the population benefited most from these improvements. In a well-known passage of his *Autobiography* Edward Gibbon says:

'The death of a new-born child before that of its parents may seem an unnatural, but it is strictly a probable event; since of any given number, the greater part are extinguished before their ninth year, before they possess the faculties of mind or body. Without accusing the profuse waste or imperfect workmanship of Nature, I shall only observe that this unfavourable chance was multiplied against my infant existence. So feeble was my constitution, so precarious my life, that in the baptism of each of my brothers, my father's prudence repeated my Christian name of Edward, that in case of the departure of the eldest son, this patronymic appellation might be still perpetuated in the family.'

This was written in 1792–3. By that time it is probable that the profuse waste of infant life was a little less than at the date of Gibbon's birth, and, if so, there would be a higher percentage of children and young people in the population. It is a matter to be borne in mind in considering the constitution of the labour force of the early factories.

The increase of the population of Britain occurred at a time when the output of commodities was also increasing at a rapid rate, and this coincidence has led to hasty generalizations. Some writers have drawn the inference that it was the growth of industry that led to the growth of numbers. If this were true the growth of industry must have exerted its influence, not through the birth rate (which, as we have seen, remained steady), but through the death rate. Some of the improvements in the arts of living mentioned above certainly depended on a development of industry, but it would be rash to assign to this a major part in the reduction of mortality. For population was growing rapidly, not only in Britain, but also in most other countries of western and northern Europe, where nothing in the nature of an industrial revolution occurred.

Other writers, reversing the causal sequence, have declared that the growth of population, through its effect on the demand for commodities, stimulated the expansion of industry. An increase of people, however, does not necessarily mean either a greater effective demand for manufactured goods or an increased production of these in the country concerned. (If it did we should expect to find a rapid economic development of Ireland in the eighteenth, and of Egypt, India, and China in the nineteenth century.) It may just as well lead to a lower standard of life for all. The spectre of the pressure of population on the means of subsistence which oppressed the mind of Malthus in 1798 was no chimera. It is true that the immediate pressure was less than Malthus supposed. But if, after the middle of the nineteenth century, there had been no railways in America, no opening up of the prairies, and no steamships, Britain might have learnt from bitter experience the fallacy of the view that, because with every pair of hands there is a mouth, therefore every expansion of numbers must lead to an increase of consumption and so of output. In Britain, in the eighteenth century and later, it so happened that, alongside the increase of population, there was taking place an increase of the other factors of production, and hence it was possible for the standard of life of the people—or of most of them—to rise.

There was an increase in the acreage of land under

cultivation. Much attention was given to the draining of fens and marshes, to the breaking up and turning to arable of the old, rough, common pastures (which were usually spoken of as the waste), and to the hedging of land, so as to make it more productive of both crops and livestock. 'In this manner', wrote an observer of these developments, 'was more useful territory added to the empire, at the expence of individuals, than had been gained by every war since the Revolution.' Several new crops were introduced. The turnip made it possible to increase the size of the herds of cattle, and the potato, which was becoming a popular food in the North, brought substantial economies in the use of land. More will be said later about the agricultural and agrarian changes. It is sufficient here to make the point that land previously outside the system of economic activities was being drawn in, and put to better use. The lines of the moving frontier can be discerned on the hillsides to-day by those with eyes to see.

At the same time there was taking place a rapid increase of capital. The number of people with incomes more than sufficient to cover the primary needs of life was growing: the power to save was increasing. Stable political and social conditions, following the settlement of 1688, encouraged men to look to more distant horizons: what economists call time-preference was favourable to accumulation. The class structure also was favourable to it. It is generally recognized that more saving takes place in communities in which the distribution of wealth is uneven than in those in which it approaches more closely to modern conceptions of what is just. Estimates of statisticians, from Gregory King in 1688 to Colquhoun in 1812, exhibit wide variations in the incomes of different social classes; and the rise of new institutions, including that of the National Debt, intensified the disparities that had been handed down from earlier generations.

The public debt, as we know it to-day, arose out of the exigencies of the wars of William III. It grew steadily—almost entirely as the result of successive wars—until, by 1815, it had reached a figure of £861 millions. Not all of it was held by the British people themselves: in 1776, it was estimated, about three-sevenths of it was in the hands of the Dutch. But, after 1781, when Holland became involved in war with Britain, the great bulk of the debt came to be held in this country—by noblemen, squires, lawyers, retired merchants, and widows and spinsters of the well-to-do classes. In 1815 perhaps about one-eleventh, and in 1827 (according to the estimate of Sir Henry Parnell) one-twelfth, of the money income of the people of the United Kingdom consisted of sums raised from the taxpayers, including the poor, and transferred to the relatively rich holders of government bonds. In this way, increasingly, wealth came into the hands of those whose propensity was to save, rather than to spend.

Accumulation does not of itself, however, lead to the creation of capital goods: it was not only a willingness to save, but also a willingness to employ savings productively, that increased at this time. In the early eighteenth century, landlords had used saved resources to improve their own estates, merchants to extend their markets, and manufacturers to engage more labour; and some of the savings of the retired and leisured classes had been lent on mortgage to local landowners, farmers or tradesmen, or invested in the shares of a turnpike trust.

Gradually the market for capital widened, aided by the rise of country bankers (who existed long before they took the name). The offer by the State of a mass of gilt-edged stock accustomed men to the idea of impersonal investment, and so they came to put their savings into enterprises distant in space and speculative in character. That the results might not always be advantageous was made manifest when the South Sea Bubble burst in 1720 and brought ruin to thousands. But, in general, the increased mobility of capital was socially beneficial, leading as it did to a substantial fall in the rate of interest.

For centuries the attitude of the State to the taking of interest had been one of hostility or, at least, of suspicion. The State was an habitual debtor—and laws had been passed prohibiting the making of loans at more than a prescribed rate. In 1625 the legal rate had been lowered from 10 to 8 per cent.; in 1651 it was reduced to 6, and in 1714 to 5—in each case following upon a fall in the 'natural' rate. In the early eighteenth century the abundance of loanable funds made it possible for finance ministers to reduce the interest paid to the creditors of the State. During the wars, the Government of William III had been obliged to offer 7 or 8 per cent. (the Usury Laws did not apply to the State); but in 1717 the rate on the perpetual annuities was reduced to 5, and in 1727 to 4 per cent. Finally, in the 1750s, Pelham lowered it once more, and, by converting a number of issues into a single one, brought into being, in 1757, the 3 per cent. Consolidated Stock which, for short, we call Consols. These conversions were not imposed on an unwilling public: they reflected, rather than initiated, a fall of the rate of interest in the community generally.

B

There was, at this period, no single market rate to which reference can be made, but the process can be observed in the rising price of Bank of England stock; and the ledgers of merchants and manufacturers afford further evidence of what was taking place. Much economic activity at this time was controlled by small groups of partners, each of whom was entitled either to receive his share of the annual profits or to leave it, wholly or in part, to earn interest in the concern. During the early part of the eighteenth century the rate allowed on money reinvested in this way was falling steadily. A firm of ironmasters of Worcestershire, Edward Knight and Company, for example, credited each partner with 5 per cent. on the undistributed profit during the 'twenties and early 'thirties, but in 1735 the rate was reduced to 4, and in 1756 to as little as 3 per cent. If a group of men were considering the investment of their savings in some new, large capital enterprise, such as a turnpike, they would first make an estimate of the number of years it would take for their capital to be restored to them in full. If the current rate of interest were 5 per cent. it would be worth while embarking on an undertaking that would return the capital in twenty years; at 4 per cent. investment might be extended to one that would take twenty-five years, and at 3 per cent. to one that would take up to thirty-three and a third years, to reimburse the initial outlay. The lower the rate at which capital could be obtained—the smaller the advantage forgone in locking it up in a fixed form—the further would capital works be extended.

As early as 1668 Sir Josiah Child remarked that 'all countries are at this day richer or poorer in an exact proportion to what they pay, and have usually paid, for the

Interest of Money'. He went on to observe that 'the bringing down of Interest from 6 to 4, or 3 per cent. will necessarily . . . double the Capital Stock of the Nation' and added that 'the Nobility and Gentry, whose estates lie mostly in Land, may presently upon all they have, instead of fifty write one hundred'. In spite of this early exposition of the relation between interest, capital, and well-being, the importance of the lowering of the rate of interest in the half-century before the industrial revolution has never been properly stressed by historians. If we seek—it would be wrong to do so—for a single reason why the pace of economic development quickened about the middle of the eighteenth century, it is to this we must look. The deep mines, solidly built factories, well-constructed canals, and substantial houses of the industrial revolution were the products of relatively cheap capital.

One thing more was necessary: the increasing supplies of labour, land, and capital had to be co-ordinated. The eighteenth and early nineteenth centuries were rich in entrepreneurs, quick to devise new combinations of productive factors, eager to find new markets, receptive to new ideas. 'The age is running mad after innovation', said Dr. Johnson; 'all the business of the world is to be done in a new way; men are to be hanged in a new way; Tyburn itself is not safe from the fury of innovation.' The sentiments and attitudes of mind of the period were propitious. The religious and political differences that had torn society apart in the two preceding centuries had been composed; and if the eighteenth century was not markedly an age of faith, at least it practised the Christian virtue of tolerance. The regulation of industry by gilds, municipalities, and the central government had broken down or had been allowed to sleep, and the field was open for the exercise of initiative and enterprise. It was perhaps no accident that it was in Lancashire and the West Riding, which had been exempted from some of the more restrictive provisions of the Elizabethan code of industrial legislation, that the development was most marked. It was certainly no accident that it was the villages and unincorporated towns—places like Manchester and Birmingham—that grew most rapidly, for industry and trade had long been moving away from the areas where some remnants of public control were still in operation.

During the seventeenth century the attitude of the Law had changed: from the time of Coke judgements in the courts of Common Law had become tender indeed to the rights of property, but hostile to privilege. In 1624 the Statute of Monopolies had swept away many vested interests, and a century and a half later Adam Smith was able to say of Englishmen that they were 'to their great honour of all peoples, the least subject to the wretched spirit of monopoly'. Whether or not the patent system, the lines of which had been laid down by that same Statute, was stimulating to innovation in industrial practice is not easy to determine. It gave security to the inventor, but it allowed some privileged positions to be maintained for an undue length of time, and it was sometimes used to block the way to new contrivance: for nearly a quarter of a century, for example, James Watt was able to prevent other engineers from constructing new types of steam engine, even under licence from himself. Many manufacturers—not all from disinterested motives—opposed the application of the law and encouraged piracy. Associations were brought into being in

Manchester and other centres of industry to contest the legality of rights claimed by patentees. The Society for the Encouragement of Arts, Manufactures and Commerce, founded in 1754, offered premiums to inventors who were willing to put their devices at the free disposal of all. And Parliament itself made awards (for example, £14,000 to Thomas Lombe when his patent for silk-throwing expired, £30,000 to Jenner for the discovery of vaccine inoculation, £10,000 to Edmund Cartwright for various contrivances, and £5,000 to Samuel Crompton for his invention of the 'mule') in addition to the substantial annual grants it voted for the use of the Board of Agriculture and the Veterinary College. Without any such monetary incentive, one of the outstanding industrialists, Josiah Wedgwood, resolved 'to be released from these degrading slavish chains, these mean, selfish fears of other people copying my works'; and, at a later stage, the inventors of the safety lamps, Sir Humphry Davy, Dr. Clanny, and George Stephenson, all refused, in the interest of the miners, to take out patents for their devices. It is at least possible that without the apparatus of the patent system discovery might have developed quite as rapidly as it did.

Some accounts of the technological revolution begin with the story of a dreamy boy watching the steam raise the lid of the kettle on the domestic hearth, or with that of a poor weaver gazing with stupefaction at his wife's spinning wheel, overturned on the floor but still revolving. These, needless to say, are nothing but romantic fiction. Other accounts leave the impression that the inventions were the work of obscure millwrights, carpenters, or clockmakers, untutored in principles, who stumbled by chance on some device that was destined to bring others to fame and fortune and themselves to penury. It is true that there were inventors—men like Brindley and Murdoch—who were endowed with little learning, but with much native wit. It is true that there were others, such as Crompton and Cort, whose discoveries transformed whole industries, but left them to end their days in relative poverty. It is true that a few new products came into being as the result of accident. But such accounts have done harm by obscuring the fact that systematic thought lay behind most of the innovations in industrial practice, by making it appear that the distribution of rewards and penalties in the economic system was wholly irrational, and, above all, by over-stressing the part played by chance in technical progress. 'Chance', as Pasteur said, 'favours only the mind which is prepared': most discoveries are achieved only after repeated trial and error. Many involve two or more previously independent ideas or processes, which, brought together in the mind of the inventor, issue in a more or less complex and efficient mechanism. In this way, for example, the principle of the jenny was united by Crompton with that of spinning by rollers to produce the mule; and the iron rail, which had long been in use in the coal mine, was joined to the locomotive to create the railway. In such cases of what has been called cross-mutation the part played by chance must have been very small indeed.

Yet other accounts of the industrial revolution are misleading because they present discovery as the achievement of individual genius, and not as a social process. 'Invention', as a distinguished modern scientist, Michael Polanyi, has remarked, 'is a drama enacted on a crowded stage.' The applause tends to be given to those who happen to be on the boards in the final act, but the success of the performance depends on the close co-operation of many players, and of those behind the scenes. The men who, together, whether as rivals or as associates, created the technique of the industrial revolution were plain Englishmen or Scots,

Being neither demigods nor heroes,
But ingenious, hard-working descendants of *homo sapiens*,
Who had the luck to plant their seedlings in fine weather,
Not in the frost or storm, but when the slow ripening of time, the felicitous crossing of circumstance
Presented unimagined opportunities,
Which they seized. . . .

(The words are those of a master cotton-spinner, Godfrey Armitage, of our own day.)

Invention appears at every stage of human history, but it rarely thrives in a community of simple peasants or unskilled manual labourers: only when division of labour has developed, so that men devote themselves to a single product or process, does it come to harvest. Such division of labour already existed when the eighteenth century opened, and the industrial revolution was in part cause, and in part effect, of a heightening and extension of the principle of specialization.

Invention, again, is more likely to arise in a community that sets store by things of the mind than in one that seeks only material ends. The stream of English scientific thought, issuing from the teaching of Francis Bacon, and enlarged by the genius of Boyle and Newton, was one of the main tributaries of the industrial revolution. Newton, indeed, was too good a philosopher and scholar to care whether or not the ideas he gave to the world were immediately 'useful'; but the belief in the possibility of achieving industrial progress by the method of observation and experiment came to the eighteenth century largely through him. Natural philosophy was shaking itself free from its association with metaphysics and—again the application of the principle of division of labour—splitting up into the separate systems of physiology, chemistry, physics, geology and so on. The sciences were not, however, as yet so specialized as to be out of contact with the language, thought, and practice of ordinary men. It was as a result of a visit to Norfolk, where he had gone to study the new methods of farming, that the Scottish landowner, James Hutton, became interested in the constitution of soils; and the discoveries that made him the most famous geologist of his day owed something to the navvies who were cutting the clays and blasting the rock to provide England with canals. Physicists and chemists, such as Franklin, Black, Priestley, Dalton, and Davy, were in intimate contact with the leading figures in British industry: there was much coming and going between the laboratory and the workshop, and men like James Watt, Josiah Wedgwood, William Reynolds, and James Keir were at home in the one as in the other. The names of engineers, ironmasters, industrial chemists, and instrument-makers on the list of Fellows of the Royal Society show how close were the relations between science and practice at this time.

Inventors, contrivers, industrialists, and entrepreneurs—it is not easy to distinguish one from another at a period of rapid change—came from every social class and from all parts of the country. Aristocrats, like Lord Lovell, in the early part of the century, and Coke of Holkham in the later, initiated improvements in agriculture; others, such as the Duke of Bridgewater and Earl Gower, created new forms of transport; and yet others were responsible for innovations in the chemical and mining industries. Clergymen and parsons, including Edmund Cartwright and Joseph Dawson, forsook the cure of souls to find out more efficient ways of weaving cloth and smelting iron. Doctors of medicine, among whom were John Roebuck and James Keir, took to chemical research and became captains of large-scale industry. Under the influence of a rationalist philosophy, scholars turned from the humanities to physical science, and some from physical science to technology. Lawyers, soldiers, public servants, and men of humbler station than these found in manufacture possibilities of advancement far greater than those offered in their original callings. A barber, Richard Arkwright, became the wealthiest and most influential of the cotton-spinners; an innkeeper, Peter Stubs, built up a highly esteemed concern in the file trade; a schoolmaster, Samuel Walker, became the leading figure in the north of England iron industry. 'Every man', exclaimed the ebullient William Hutton in 1780, 'has his fortune in his own hands.' That, it is needless to say, has never been true, or even half true; but anyone who looks closely at English society in the mid- and late eighteenth century will understand how it was possible for it to be said, for at this time vertical mobility had reached a degree higher than that of any earlier, or perhaps any succeeding, age.

It has often been observed that the growth of industry was connected historically with the rise of groups which dissented from the Church by law established in England. In the seventeenth century the congregation of Puritans gathered about Richard Baxter at Kidderminster included the Foleys, the Crowleys, and the

Hanburys, who were to set up great establishments in places as far afield as Staffordshire, Durham, and South Wales. In the following century members of the Society of Friends played a prominent part in the development of corn-milling, brewing, pharmacy, and banking; and the Quaker families of the Darbys, Reynolds, Lloyds, and Huntsmans came to direct the destinies of the iron and steel industries at a period of rapid change. There were Baptists, like Thomas Newcomen, and Presbyterians, like James Watt, in engineering; Congregationalists, like John Roebuck and Joseph Dawson, alongside the Quakers, in iron-smelting; and Unitarians, including the M'Connels and the Gregs, in cotton-spinning. In cotton, moreover, the greatest inventor, Samuel Crompton, was a disciple of Emmanuel Swedenborg—who himself, it may be recalled, was an authority on metals and the technique of mines. Other industrialists, among whom were the Guests of South Wales, drew strength from the teaching of John Wesley. But Wesley's first appeal was to the poor and unprivileged, and the effects of Methodism are to be seen less in the quickening of enterprise than in the greater sobriety, diligence and self-discipline of the workers who came under its influence.

Many explanations have been offered of this close association between industry and Dissent. It has been suggested that those who sought out new forms of worship would also naturally strike out new paths in secular fields. It has been argued that there is an intimate connexion between the tenets peculiar to Nonconformity and the rules of conduct that lead to success in business. And it has been asserted that the exclusion of Dissenters from the universities, and from office in government and administration, forced many to seek an outlet for their abilities in industry and trade. There may be something in each of these contentions, but a simpler explanation lies in the fact that, broadly speaking, the Nonconformists constituted the better educated section of the middle classes. This view is supported by a consideration of the part played in the economic movement by the stream of energy that poured into England from Presbyterian Scotland after (though not immediately after) the Union of 1707. The greatest inventor of the age, James Watt, came from Scotland, as also did seven of his eight assistants in the business of erecting engines. Sir John Sinclair, Thomas Telford, John Macadam, David Mushet, and James Beaumont Neilson brought their Scottish vigour of mind and character to English agriculture, transport, and iron-making. Highlanders and Lowlanders, alike, tramped to the Lancashire cotton area, many of them pausing at the little village of Chowbent, where a fellow countryman named Cannan directed them to centres which offered scope for their several abilities. Among those who took the southern road to fortune in textiles were James McGuffog, James M'Connel, John Kennedy, George and Adam Murray and—bearers of names that are honoured to-day, not only in Lancashire—John Gladstone and Henry Bannerman. These and other immigrants were not illiterate peasants. Some were sons of the manse, and even those of humbler station had been given at least the rudiments of a sound education in the village or burgh school of their native place.

If the Scottish system of primary education was in advance of that of any other European country at this time, the same was true of the Scottish universities. It was not from Oxford or Cambridge, where the torch burnt dim, but from Glasgow and Edinburgh, that the impulse to scientific inquiry and its practical application came. Many young men, attracted by the learning and personality of Joseph Black, Professor of Chemistry at Glasgow and later at Edinburgh, were trained to methods of thought and experiment which were afterwards directed to industrial ends. Among them was James Keir, a pioneer in the chemical and glass industries, and (if the circle may be extended to those who were not formally students of Black, but owed much to his teaching and friendship) John Roebuck, James Watt, and Alexander Cochrane, the brilliant but unfortunate Earl of Dundonald.

In a humbler way the academies established by nonconformist zeal for education—at Bristol, Manchester, Northampton, Daventry, Warrington and elsewhere— did for England in the eighteenth century something of what the universities did for Scotland. Open to all, irrespective of creed, they provided a curriculum which, weighted, it is true, with Divinity, Rhetoric and Jewish Antiquities, included Mathematics, History, Geography, French, and Bookkeeping. Among their pupils were Daniel Defoe (and a contemporary named Cruso), John Cope, John Howard, Thomas Malthus, and William Hazlitt—to name only a few of those who were to rise to distinction in letters and public life. What is more to our immediate purpose, they were nurseries of scientific thought. Several of them were well equipped with 'philosophical instruments' and offered facilities for experiment : their teachers included men of the quality of Joseph Priestley and John Dalton; and from them proceeded a stream of future industrialists, among whom were John Roebuck (who was trained at Northampton before proceeding to Edinburgh and Leyden), Matthew Boulton, John Wilkinson, Benjamin Gott, and—of a later generation—Joseph Whitworth.

Apart from the dissenting academies, there were in many towns institutions which, like the national Society of Arts, were devoted to the improvement of methods of production. Informal groups of scientists and manufacturers came into being in Lancashire and the Midlands, as well as at Edinburgh and Glasgow. Who can say how much the master cotton-spinners gained from their contact with Thomas Percival and John Dalton in the Literary and Philosophical Society of Manchester; or how much Birmingham and its province owes to the Lunar Society, in which Erasmus Darwin, R. L. Edgeworth, Joseph Priestley, James Watt, Matthew Boulton, and Josiah Wedgwood brought their powerful minds to bear on the problems of life and, no less, on those of getting a living?

The conjuncture of growing supplies of land, labour, and capital made possible the expansion of industry; coal and steam provided the fuel and power for large-scale manufacture; low rates of interest, rising prices, and high expectations of profit offered the incentive. But behind and beyond these material and economic factors lay something more. Trade with foreign parts had widened men's views of the world, and science their conception of the universe: the industrial revolution was also a revolution of ideas. If it registered an advance in understanding of, and control over, Nature, it also saw the beginning of a new attitude to the problems of human society. And here, again, it was from Scotland, and the University of Glasgow in particular, that the clearest beam of light was thrown. The 'Commonsense School', with its empiricism, its optimism, and its ethics of enlightened self-interest, provided a system of doctrine agreeable to the more philosophically-minded of the men of action who carried the industrial movement to its triumph. It is, no doubt, an academic error to overstress the part played by speculative thought in shaping the lives of ordinary men and women: it is arguable that John Wesley, Tom Paine, William Cobbett, and Orator Hunt were of as much immediate consequence as David Hume, or even Jeremy Bentham. But, at least, there is one product of the Scottish school of moral philosophy that cannot pass without mention in any account of the forces that produced the industrial revolution. The *Enquiry into the Nature and Causes of the Wealth of Nations*, which appeared in 1776, was to serve as a court of appeal on matters of economics and politics for generations to come. Its judgements were the material from which men not given to the study of treatises framed their maxims of conduct for business and government alike. It was under its influence that the idea of a more or less fixed volume of trade and employment, directed and regulated by the State, gave way—gradually and with many setbacks—to thoughts of unlimited progress in a free and expanding economy.

CHAPTER II

THE EARLIER FORMS OF INDUSTRY

I

In the eighteenth century most of the people of Britain earned their living by work on the land. Conditions of life and labour varied with each small difference of configuration, sub-soil and climate. But, apart from such diversities, there was one broad contrast that could hardly fail to impress itself on every traveller who rode through the English shires : that between the areas where the fields lay open, stretching unbroken to the horizon, and those where they were divided by quickset hedges, stone walls, fences, or rows of trees.

The open-field village, with its hierarchy of lord or squire, freeholders, copyholders, leaseholders, and cottagers, was well suited to the needs of a community producing grain and a small amount of livestock for its own subsistence. But, though it was more adaptable than has sometimes been supposed, it tended to hold by the methods of cultivation and economic relations of the past. Before a system of drainage or a new rotation of crops could be introduced it was necessary to win the assent of a body of men most of whom were satisfied with customary practice and suspicious of change. Progress in agriculture was bound up with the creation of new units of administration in which the individual had more scope for experiment; and this meant the parcelling out and enclosure of the common fields, or the breaking up of the rough pasture and waste which had previously contributed little to the output of the village.

Enclosure had been taking place almost continuously from at least as early as the thirteenth century. Its development had been connected with production, not for subsistence, but for the market. In Tudor and Stuart times much of it had been for the purpose of supplying wool to the expanding textile industry; and, even in the half-century after 1700, the enclosures were most often in regions specially suited to pasture. It was the growing demand for wool and leather, rather than for grain, that provided the incentive.

The process was closely associated with the concentration of ownership into fewer hands. It was not that there was any pressing need for larger farms: many of the holdings in the open fields were quite big enough to be efficient units of production. But when a single lord, or a few substantial squires, came to control an area it was easy to bring about changes of method, whether on a compact home farm, or indirectly through conditions imposed on the leaseholders, who were coming to take the place of the freeholders or customary tenants of the older system.

Many of the earlier enclosures had been carried out by men who had made their fortunes in trade or in government service and who sought the prestige that, in England, has always gone with the possession of the soil. But in the first half of the eighteenth century the old landed aristocracy, which had lost much in the Civil Wars, was reasserting its claims to its former place in society. Noblemen were making much use of entail, so as to keep their properties intact. Encouraged by low rates of interest, they were mortgaging their estates and using the proceeds to buy more land. Above all, they were initiating enclosures. Most of these were made by private arrangements between the proprietors concerned: they took place in parishes where the number of owners was small and the average holding correspondingly large, and these were generally the ones in which pasture was a prominent activity. Where the land was in many hands it was often necessary to buy out the freeholders: the disappearance of the yeoman, about which much has been written, was not generally a result of the enclosure but a prelude to it. If the freeholders proved obdurate it was possible to obtain Parliamentary powers to give effect to the wishes of those, however few in number, who controlled the greater part of the soil. But enclosure by Act did not play an important part until after 1760: many of the yeomen seem to have been willing to sell their small freeholds and to use the money to set up as large leasehold farmers; and some (there can be little doubt) transferred their capital and energies to manufacture.

There were, however, humbler classes of people who received little or no consideration. The cottagers, who had cultivated a few strips in the open fields, and supplemented their incomes by part-time work on those of their wealthier neighbours, might, indeed, be given a small holding when the land was re-divided. But it was less easy to graze a cow, keep fowls, or gather fuel, when the greater part of the waste had been allotted to the squire or the larger cultivators. On the fringe of most open-field villages, there were many squatters who obtained a precarious living, either by primitive husbandry on tiny intakes, or by wage-earning, poaching, begging, thieving, or the receipt of poor relief. Taking little

c

part in the life of the community, they had been tolerated by the easy-going, open-field cultivators. But the enclosed village had little use for such people: their presence was an obstacle to the full utilization of the land, and their poverty laid a burden of parish rates on the tenant farmers. Evicted from their cottages, which were afterwards razed to the ground, they crowded to areas where the fields were still open, or took to vagrancy. They and their descendants must have contributed largely to the body of semi-employed, inefficient labour that was to trouble the peace of politicians and poor-law administrators until 1834, and beyond.

Some writers who have dwelt at length on the fate of those who were forced to leave the land have tended to overlook the constructive activities that were being carried on inside the fences. The essential fact about enclosure is that it brought about an increase in the productivity of the soil. There has been much discussion as to whether it led to a decline in the number of cultivators, and some who hold that it did write as though this were a consequence to be deplored. It is a truism, however, that the standard of life of a nation is raised when fewer people are needed to provide the means of subsistence. Many of those who were divorced from the soil (as the stereotyped phrase goes) were free to devote themselves to other activities: it was precisely because enclosure released (or drove) men from the land that it is to be counted among the processes that led to the industrial revolution, with the higher standards of consumption that this brought with it.

The enclosures were initiated by 'spirited landowners' many of whom adhered to some particular school of agricultural doctrine or practice. Among the most

celebrated of the reformers was Jethro Tull (1674–1741), *Tull.*
a law student who, at the age of twenty-five, took to farming with considerable success. Tull held to a peculiar
theory of cultivation. Believing that plants could obtain
nutriment only in the form of tiny particles, which he
called atoms, he advocated a constant pulverization of
the soil by deep working; and to facilitate this he invented, or developed, in 1714, a horse-drawn hoe. In
many respects his teaching was retrograde. He was an
opponent of the use of manures. His practice of sowing
in drills, wide apart, was economical of seed, but wasteful
of land. And his hostility to rotation (supported as it
was by a claim to have grown wheat for thirteen successive years on the same land) set back the movement to
progressive farming in many parts of England. Tull was
a crank, and his importance in the history of agriculture
has been vastly exaggerated. It was not from his farms
in Berkshire, but from those of the large-scale proprietors
of Norfolk, that the real innovations came.

What is known as the Norfolk system was (as an
American, Naomi Riches, has said) a series of interre-
lated technical, economic and legal processes, combined
on an enclosed farm. It included the introduction to
sandy soils of marl and clay, the rotation of crops, the
growing of turnips, clover and new grasses, the production of grain and cattle rather than of sheep, and
cultivation by tenants, under long leases, on large-scale
holdings. Some of its features were derived from Continental example; for Norfolk, with its textile and fishing
trades, had close connexions with the Netherlands. But
most of them were the product of an indigenous race of
energetic landlords and cultivators. Lord Lovell (1697–
1755), predecessor and relative of the famous Coke of

Holkham, was active in the use of marls, the draining of marshes, and the practice of rotation; and the name of Viscount Townshend (1674–1738) has been connected with the introduction of the turnip as a field crop, though recent research has shown that he was the popularizer, rather than the originator of this. But the Norfolk system, like every major innovation, was the work of many hands and brains. Much of the history of agriculture in the eighteenth century is concerned with the spread to other parts of Britain of its four-course rotation (turnips, barley, clover, wheat, or some variant of this) in place of the three-course (spring crop, winter crop and fallow) of the old Midlands system. The cultivation of grasses and turnips meant that areas of what had been permanent pasture could be brought under the plough; and, since cattle could now be maintained through the winter, the supply of natural fertilizer for the cereal and root crops was increased. But the transition to 'convertible husbandry' was very slow: the open-field system, with its concentration on grain, rather than livestock, died hard. In no part of Britain—not even in Norfolk itself—were the innovations adopted on such a scale as to make it possible to speak of an agricultural, or an agrarian, revolution.

In all parts of the world textiles have been one of the earliest offshoots of a peasant economy. In Britain wool from the backs of sheep had, for many generations, provided the material for an activity second only to agriculture in the number of people it employed and the volume of trade it supported. The importance of this industry in the eyes of government is attested by a long list of measures which sought to prevent the export of raw wool, the emigration of skilled workers, and the import of fabrics that might compete with woollen cloths in the home market. People were exhorted, or constrained, to dress in English materials, and even the dead were not allowed to be buried in any fabric other than wool.

Production consisted of a long chain of processes. First the wool was sorted, cleaned and sometimes dyed. Next it was either combed, to separate the long hairs from the short, or carded, to make a fleecy roll with the fibres lying roughly parallel. After this it was spun, woven, fulled, washed, tentered (or stretched), bleached, dressed and sheared. These processes called for different degrees of skill and strength: women and children could do the sorting, cleaning and spinning, but combing, weaving, and the later operations were men's work. Some of them were performed with the aid of simple apparatus in the home. But fulling (in which the cloth was treated with fuller's earth and beaten with heavy hammers to mat the texture) was conducted in mills worked by horses or water power; dressing, or raising the nap, was done in gig mills; and dyeing needed vats and other equipment too large to be housed in a cottage.

There was probably no county of England and Wales in which woollen cloth was not produced by the part-time work of peasants, farmers, and agricultural labourers. But there were areas of concentration in the West Country, East Anglia, and Yorkshire, where men and women had become specialist spinners or weavers, thinking first of wool, treating work on the land as, at most, a by-occupation, and making yarn and cloth far superior to anything that could be produced by the rough-handed peasant.

The organization of the industry was complex, and

varied from place to place. In the West Country the well-to-do clothier gave out wool to carders and spinners, and yarn to weavers, all of whom worked in their own homes; and the undressed cloth was then passed to fullers, dressers, and shearmen, who finished it in small mills or workshops under his supervision. In East Anglia there were master-combers who controlled the work of the spinners and weavers, and merchants who directed that of the finishers. In the West Riding the clothier was often a man of quite small capital, who, aided by his family and a few apprentices or journeymen, himself wove cloth in a workshop attached to his home, using yarn spun by women in the cottages. But there were also wealthy worsted manufacturers here who gave out work by the piece to spinners, weavers and others who worked for wages. Some clothiers sold their wares direct to merchants or to customers abroad; some disposed of them through factors at Blackwell Hall in London; some took them to the annual Sturbridge Fair at Cambridge; and the Yorkshire clothier-weavers carried their un-dressed webs to weekly markets held at Halifax, Wake-field, Leeds, and Bradford.

Other branches of textiles depended for their raw materials partly, at least, on foreign sources of supply. Raw silk and organzine (thrown silk) were brought from China, Italy, Spain, and Turkey, flax from Ireland, the Baltic and North America, and cotton from the Levant and the West Indies. The manufacture of these was carried on under conditions similar in essentials to those in the woollen industry. The silk weavers tended to con-centrate in towns, at Spitalfields, Coventry, Norwich, and Macclesfield. They worked in garrets or sheds in each of which perhaps half a dozen looms were controlled by a capitalist employer. The manufacture of linen and cotton was more widely scattered, but there was a strong tendency to localization in Lancashire and the Lowlands of Scotland. Cotton was too short in staple to be used as warp, except in the production of small fabrics, such as handkerchiefs: hence what was later to become by far the greatest centre of textile production had to depend for its yarn largely on linen and wool, and only to a less extent on cotton. The typical products of Lancashire in the first half of the eighteenth century were pure woollens, cotton-linen fustians and checks, and smallwares (including tapes, braid, ribbons, incles and thread) made of such diverse materials as cotton, linen, silk, worsted, and mohair.

The organization of the textile manufactures of Lancashire cannot be described in a few words. Suffice it to say that the central figure was a merchant, clothier, or linen-draper, who employed putters-out to distribute material, either direct to the scattered spinners and weavers, or to country manufacturers who, in turn, put it out in their own areas. There were some farmer-weavers, who divided their energies between the plough and the loom. But most of the weavers, even in the country, were virtually full-time operatives; and in the larger towns, like Manchester, where smallwares were produced on expensive Dutch looms, the workers were entirely dependent on the capital of the merchants and linen-drapers who not only provided the material, but often owned the bleach-crofts, dye-houses, and work-shops where the finishing processes were performed.

The clothing, as distinct from the textile, trades were relatively small and unimportant, for most families made their own garments or employed sempstresses who

worked for wretchedly low wages. Beaver hats had long
been made in London; felt hats, of rabbit skin and other
material, were produced in many places, including
Stockport and Manchester; and straw plaiting and straw
hat-making gave rise to a cottage industry, conducted
mainly by women and children in their own homes,
in Bedfordshire, Buckinghamshire, and Hertfordshire.
Stockings were still knitted by hand in cottages, especially in Scotland and Wales, where there were fairs
specialized to their sale; but from the days of Elizabeth,
when a cleric, William Lee, had invented a stocking-
frame, many men, women and children in London had
found employment in frame-work knitting. In the early
eighteenth century the industry was moving from the
Metropolis to the counties of Derby, Nottingham, and
Leicester, where control by the Framework Knitters'
Company was ineffective, and where labour was cheap.
The hosier, who owned the frames, usually kept a few
at his own shop or warehouse, but most of them were
hired to knitters who worked in their homes, on yarn of
varied materials brought to their doors by putters-out.
Before the middle of the century there were Midland
hosiers who owned as many as a hundred frames, and a
new class of master-stockingers had begun to act as intermediaries between them and the knitters. Originally
putters-out, these men entered into contracts with the
hosiers for work which they gave out at piece-rates, and
also hired frames which they sub-let, at increased rents,
to the knitters. Though the hosier continued to own
both the material and the frames, he had become little
more than a merchant, without direct relations with
those who depended on him for employment.

Even in the first half of the eighteenth century,

1750

however, there were portents of change in the textile industries. Here and there, for technical reasons, small groups of men were being brought together into workshops and little water-driven mills. There was much innovation and experiment. In 1717 Thomas Lombe, whose brother had brought designs of machines from Italy, set up a true factory on the River Derwent, where nearly 300 workmen were employed in throwing silk. It was the precursor of a host of similar factories—though of few in silk manufacture, which has never, indeed, found Britain congenial to its growth. In 1733 a Lancashire clock-maker, John Kay, made a simple, but important, improvement in the loom, by which the shuttle, mounted on wheels, was struck by hammers and so driven through the warp. The fly-shuttle was a labour-saving device: it enabled a single weaver, sitting at the loom and holding in his hand strings attached to the hammers, to make cloth of a width that had previously required the work of two men. But the device encountered opposition from the Lancashire weavers, and there were probably mechanical difficulties that were only slowly overcome: it was not until after 1760 that the fly-shuttle came into general use. In 1738 Lewis Paul of Birmingham, the son of a physician, hit on an idea which was to do for spinning what Kay's device was ultimately to do for weaving. The carded cotton or wool was passed through two sets of rollers, revolving at different speeds, and in this way was drawn out before it passed to the spindle which gave the twist. But attempts to make use of the contrivance in small mills at Birmingham, London, Northampton and Leominster all failed, partly, it would appear, because of technical defects, but also perhaps (as Paul said) because of the poor quality and shiftless habits of the workers. It was not until nearly two generations later, when Arkwright took up the idea, that roller spinning was able to transform the methods of producing yarn, and so virtually to create an industry based solely on cotton, and conducted in factories.

The other leading industries of Britain were all, like textiles, in one way or another, closely connected with agriculture. This was true, in particular, of the mining of coal. It was the owners of the land who controlled the working of the underground seams and drew from them their rents and royalties. Coal-mining was carried on in a rural rather than an urban setting: it made use of large numbers of horses for winding and transport, and to maintain these most colliery owners kept farms on which they grew oats and other crops. The colliers themselves were close to the soil: it was usual for them to leave the pits for work on the land in the months of harvest; and the methods of hiring, and relations with employers, were very similar to those of the agricultural labourer.

At the beginning of the eighteenth century most of the coalfields had long passed the stage of outcrop, or pit-and-adit mining. Shafts were sunk, sometimes to a depth of 200 feet or more; underground galleries were extensive; and primitive systems of ventilation had been devised. Access by sea to the London market made the Northumberland and Durham coalfield by far the largest and best developed area of production. Here landed proprietors and other capitalists formed partnerships or companies, employed expert 'viewers' to give advice on the conduct of their operations, and appointed overmen at the separate pits to control the undermen who supervised the work of the hewers and barrowmen. In most other coalfields there was no such hierarchy of officials: the working colliers formed themselves into companies, of six or eight or a dozen men, and made contracts through their leader (a charter-master or butty) either to work the whole of a small pit, to get and carry to the customer a certain amount of coal, or to drive a certain length of underground way, for an agreed sum.

This difference of organization was associated with a difference in the manner of working the coal. In Northumberland and Durham, Cumberland, Lancashire, and Scotland, the method was that of the pillar and stall: the stall or bord in which the pitman hewed, assisted by a single boy, was supported by columns of coal; and as much as a half, or even two-thirds, of the mineral might be left unworked to support the roof. But in the Midlands—in Shropshire, Staffordshire, and Warwickshire—where roofs and floors were stronger, the colliers worked co-operatively by longwall, supporting the roof with props, and flinging the stone or slack behind them into the goaf from which the coal had already been worked.

There were differences also in the methods of moving the coal underground. In the northern field of England this was done by barrowmen, who dragged wooden sledges, shod with runners of ash, from the coal face to the pit bottom; but by 1750 ponies, tended by boys, were beginning to replace the men in the Newcastle area. In other places the coal was carried in baskets by youths or women; and in Fifeshire the wives and daughters of the colliers went bent under heavy loads, bearing the coal, not only along the underground passages, but by a series of ladders up the shaft to the surface. What a nineteenth-century colliery owner called 'the repugnant mode of conveying coals on the backs of ladies' continued in some districts till as late as 1842.

The chief technical problems of getting coal arose from the presence in the pits of gas and water. The inert gas, chokedamp, might be dispersed by dragging bunches of furze along the galleries, or by other simple devices. But the inflammable firedamp was a more serious matter. It was sometimes dealt with by a fireman, who, clad in leather or wet rags, carried a long pole with a lighted candle at the end, with which, at some personal risk, he exploded the gas. In the larger mines of the Newcastle area in the 1730s it was the practice to sink two shafts: an iron basket of flaming coals, suspended in one of these, caused the gas-laden air to rise, and so drew fresh supplies from the surface down the other shaft. About the same time, to avoid the danger of working by the light of candles a device, known as the steel-mill, was introduced into the Cumberland and Tyneside mines. A boy, standing by the hewer, caused a small toothed wheel to revolve against a flint, and so produced a shower of sparks, sufficient to give a dim illumination. But the use of the steel-mill was no guarantee against accidents, and at some pits the men preferred to make shift with such light as they could get from putrefying fish or pieces of phosphorescent wood.

Water presented the mining engineer or viewer with an even more intractable problem. In the northern coal-field it was the practice to line the shaft with sheepskins, covered with wooden 'tubbing', to keep back the springs that would otherwise have made it impossible to sink through the wet strata. The water that drained from the workings into the sump at the pit bottom was raised to the surface by a variety of devices, including hand-pumps and the endless chain of pots, worked by men, donkeys, or, occasionally, water-wheels or windmills. The cost of drainage was great and the incentive to find more efficient methods of removing water from the pits correspondingly strong. It was probably the needs of the metal miners of Cornwall that led Thomas Savery to devise in 1698 a pumping engine which involved the use of steam. Erected in a recess in the pit shaft, this consisted simply of a boiler and a condenser fitted with pipes, one of which ran down the shaft to the sump and the other to the surface. The vacuum created by condensation of the steam sucked the water from the sump; and injection of fresh steam from the boiler forced it up the eduction pipe to ground level. But the waste of energy involved in bringing steam into direct contact with cold water was enormous. It was to avoid this that an ironmonger of Dartmouth, Thomas Newcomen (1663–1729), invented, in 1708, an entirely different form of self-acting atmospheric engine. A great beam of timber, pivoted high above the ground on a solid piece of masonry, was given freedom to swing vertically through the arc of a circle. At one end the beam was connected to a piston which moved up and down, as steam was first injected, and then condensed, in the cylinder. These movements were transmitted to the beam, and so to the pump rods attached to its other end, by movement of which the water was drawn up a pipe in the mine shaft. Many modifications and additions were made by Newcomen and his successors. First employed at collieries in the Midlands, the contrivance was soon adopted in the northern coalfield, and by 1765 there were about 100 engines at work in the neighbourhood of the Tyne and Wear. They made possible the working of seams in and below the watery layers, and so were an important factor in increasing the output of the mines. Thomas Newcomen deserves a very special place in the gallery of the pioneers of modern technology.

The engine was a device used solely for pumping: it could not be employed in the process of winding. This was done by horse gins which drew the hazel corves, or baskets, containing the coal, to the top of the shaft. Sometimes the colliers ascended or descended in the baskets; but more often they thrust a leg through a loop in the winding rope, and, clustered together, rode the shaft, the boys sitting on the knees of the men, or simply clinging to the rope with hands and feet. Accidents, by striking the walls, or falling to the bottom of the shaft, were not infrequent.

The limits of output were set by difficulties of transport, not only underground for the individual pit, but also, on the surface, for the industry as a whole. In the North there were wagon ways, with wooden rails, from the collieries to the rivers, and about a thousand sea-going vessels of 300 or 400 tons carried the coal to distant parts. But the inland fields had to rely on transport in panniers, slung across the backs of horses, or in wagons moving along the ill-made roads. Not until better high-ways and canals came in could the market be more than local.

The getting of coal offered little opportunity for the application of mechanical devices in hewing and under-ground carriage: the struggle to wrest coal from the earth was, as it still is, very much a soldiers' battle, from which swift results are not to be expected. Estimates of production for early periods can be little better than guesses. But it seems likely that the output was about $2\frac{1}{2}$ million tons a year in 1700, and $4\frac{3}{4}$ million tons in 1750. Such figures are small compared with the round 10 million of 1800, the 16 million of 1829, and the far larger tonnages that were to follow: it was the nineteenth, rather than the eighteenth, century that was the age of coal. But, even in 1700 and 1750, fuel was basic to the development of most processes of production, and the relatively slow rate of progress in coal-mining set limits to the expansion of British industry in general.

One of the industries that made much use of fuel was the smelting and 'fining' of iron. In this case, however, the fuel was not coal, but charcoal, and here again there was close connection with the land, through the proprietors of the woods and coppices where it was produced. It was the presence of trees, rather than of iron ore, that determined the location of ironworks, for it was cheaper to move ore than wood or charcoal over long distances. In the sixteenth and seventeenth centuries a thriving iron industry had grown up in the Weald of Sussex and Kent. But the exhaustion of the forests in this region (largely because of the demands of ship-building, as well as of iron-making) had led to a decline; and by 1700 the industry was moving away to other parts of the country where woodlands still remained or new coppices could be planted.

To produce iron, the ore had first to be smelted in a blast furnace, and the molten metal run into pigs. It could then be either re-melted in a small air furnace and turned into castings, or passed to the forges where it was heated and hammered into bars of wrought iron. These in turn were sent to the slitting mills, where they were heated, passed through grooved rollers, and so drawn out and cut into rods. Cast iron was hard, but brittle: it was the material for such things as domestic pots and pans, and—a use by no means negligible in a century of many wars—some forms of ordnance. Wrought iron, with its lower carbon content, was malleable, tensile and able to withstand strain: it was used for making horseshoes, nails, picks and spades, locks and bolts, wire, and tools of all kinds.

Furnaces, forges, and slitting mills were generally separate undertakings—often, because of the limited supplies of fuel, carried on at a distance one from another, by producers independent of each other. The outstanding innovation in iron production in the early eighteenth century was the substitution of coke for charcoal in the production of pig iron and castings. For more than a century one projector after another had sought for a way of effecting this, and several patents had been taken out. These, however, represented aspirations, rather than achievements, for the sulphur in the coke was responsible for a product which was unfit for castings and which, when turned into wrought iron, was so brittle as to be unusable. It was not until 1709 that a Quaker ironmaster, Abraham Darby of Coalbrookdale in Shropshire, managed to produce pig iron of quality, smelted with coke. His success was, no doubt, connected with the fact that his furnace was a tall one and his blowing apparatus exceptionally powerful. But what was more important was that he had, close at hand, the clod coal of Shropshire, which produced a coke, unlike that from the coal of other areas, suitable for the purpose of the blast furnace. Darby's discovery was to lead to results of great importance to the future of Britain as an

industrial nation, but the full fruits came only later in
the century. The use of the process spread slowly—for
long only within the circle of Darby's family and friends.
Quaker reticence—and possibly a desire to keep the
knowledge from competitors—may have had something
to do with this, but the uses to which the coke-smelted
pig could be put were, in any case, restricted. Darby's
iron was, or was considered to be, too impure to serve
as material for the forge-master: it was only in the production of castings that mineral fuel was able to replace
charcoal.

The discovery led to a slow growth of furnaces and
foundries on the coalfields, rather than in the neighbourhood of the forests. It enabled the millwrights to get
better materials for some of their purposes, and led to a
substitution of cast for wrought iron in some commodities of common use. These results were not unimportant.
But they left the greater part of the iron industry still in
its semi-rural setting, bound for its power to the falling
stream, and for its fuel to the shrinking woodlands.

Intermediate in carbon content between cast iron, on
the one hand, and wrought iron, on the other, is steel.
This was made by putting pieces of wrought iron,
covered with charcoal, into an oven and keeping them
at a high temperature for several days. The blister steel
that resulted was then cut into small gadds, bound
together in faggots, re-heated in a furnace, and forged
into shear steel. Probably because the raw material was
iron of high quality, imported from Sweden, the making
of steel was localized about Newcastle-upon-Tyne.
Costs of production were great, and the use of steel was
confined to the making of cutlery, razors, the better
kinds of edge-tools, swords, guns, and the working parts

D

of clocks and watches. In the early 1740s, a Quaker clockmaker of Sheffield, Benjamin Huntsman, devised a process of melting blister or shear steel in small crucibles and so obtained a purer and more uniform product. His cast steel was to play a leading part in the growth of many industries, including engineering. But, as with others of these early discoveries, knowledge of the process spread slowly, and it was not until towards the end of the century that crucible steel came into extensive use.

In the manufacture, as distinct from the production of iron it was possible to make full use of mineral fuel and it was, therefore, on the coalfields that the makers of tools and agricultural implements, chains, locks and bolts, and, above all, nails, tended to congregate. The largest single area of production was in south Staffordshire and north-east Worcestershire, especially along the valleys of the Tame and Stour, where many old corn mills had been converted to the slitting of iron. An early concentration on the making of saddlery had, apparently, given rise to the production of bits, stirrups and other ironwork connected with horses at Walsall and West Bromwich; and Birmingham had already begun to specialize in the making of guns, swords, and those varied lighter wares of metal for which she was to become famous. But in the countryside, about these towns, the chief activity was the making of nails, for which the American colonies (where the houses were built of wood) provided a large and expanding market.

There was localization of the metal-working industries also in South Yorkshire and the neighbouring parts of Derbyshire: Sheffield concentrated on the best qualities of cutlery and tools, and the villages round about were engaged in the less skilled work of making scythes, sickles, and nails. At Newcastle-upon-Tyne, again, there were many cutlers, and nearby at Swalwell and Winlaton, Ambrose Crowley, who had come there from Stourbridge, set up a highly paternalistic enterprise for the production of anchors, chains, tools, and nails. At Winlaton the smiths and other master-workmen had their shops in a square, erected by Crowley, where they lived under semi-collegiate conditions, with their own chaplain, surgeon, and schoolmaster, and their own sick and superannuation fund. Such circumstances, however, were exceptional. In the West Midlands, in South Yorkshire, and in West Lancashire (where there was also a development of ironworking in the countryside between Liverpool, Wigan and Warrington) production was carried on in small shops or sheds attached to the scattered homes of the workers. Ironmongers gave out rods at their warehouses and the nailmakers and others brought back their finished product. But, at a later stage, there grew up a body of factors or foggers who performed functions similar to those of the putter-out in Lancashire or the stockinger or bagman in the East Midlands.

Iron and steel do not lend themselves so readily as textile fibres to machine methods: there was innovation in the types of product, but little in the processes of manufacture. The number of workers increased, and there was some growth of specialization. But the limits of output were set by those of the raw material; and it was not until late in the century, when it became possible to produce wrought iron with coal, that there could be any spectacular expansion of the metal-working trades.

Large-scale production required not only division of labour and specialized appliances, but also the support of an organized system of transport, commerce, and credit. According to all contemporary observers, the internal communications of Britain were far from meeting the needs of the industrialists. The roads of England, depending as they did for construction and repair on amateur surveyors and unskilled statute labour, were mostly unsuited to wheeled traffic; and an important means of land carriage was by pack-horses, which travelled, sometimes 100 or more in line, on stone causeways laid alongside, or in the middle of, the highways. When enclosures were made the opportunity was taken to widen and straighten the approaches to the villages, and in some areas turnpikes were constructed by trusts which, under an Act of 1662, were empowered to raise capital on the security of their future revenue from tolls. But there was much opposition to what was in fact an enclosure of the highroads, and the toll-bars were often broken down. It was not until after the middle of the century that the turnpike roads provided an efficient channel of communication in areas at all remote from London.

For bulky, heavy or fragile goods, the rivers and seas afforded a far cheaper and safer means of carriage. An extensive coasting trade was carried on between ports, the number of which ran into scores. Some of these, like Newcastle, Hull, and Bristol, already large, were to extend their trade enormously as time went on; others, like Whitby, Scarborough, King's Lynn, and Yarmouth, were to fall behind as the forces of the industrial revolution brought a concentration of trade hardly less intense than that of industry. Many, though not all, were situated at the mouths of navigable rivers, which, like the highways of the sea, played an important part in developing the inter-regional trade (and hence the localization of industry), which was a marked feature of the English economy in the period 1700–60. Nearly the whole of the fuel and most of the food of Londoners came to them by water: coal was loaded into keels on the Tyne, and transferred to sea-going colliers which carried it to the Pool, where it was unloaded into lighters; and grain and other produce of the Thames Valley were brought down the river in barges. On the Severn, trows laden with coal, hollow-ware, and nails from Shropshire and Worcestershire were floated down to Bristol, and dragged back upstream, with their cargoes of bar iron, clay, and West Indian produce, by gangs of powerful (but short-lived) bow-hauliers. The smaller rivers were less navigable. Some of them were obstructed by weirs and fish-garths; there were many shallows which, in times of drought, impeded navigation; and the un-social practice of throwing ballast overboard in an attempt to float over these sometimes put an end to traffic. Enlightened landowners and industrialists, especially in the North, formed companies and obtained statutory powers to widen and deepen many of the waterways. At an early date the improvement of the Salwarpe had aided the rise of Droitwich as a centre of salt production; but a later development of the Weaver led to a much more rapid growth of the Cheshire 'wiches'. The deepening of the Aire and Calder made it possible to bring to the West Riding the long-stapled wools of Lincoln and Leicestershire; and that of the Don stimulated the growth of the metal trades of Rotherham and, later, of Sheffield. In Lancashire there was exceptional activity: the Douglas navigation enabled the coals of the pits about Wigan to reach the estuary of the Ribble and the Fylde; the successive improvements of the Mersey and Irwell played a part in the growth of Liverpool as a port, and of Manchester as a centre of textile manufacture; and the canalization of the little Sankey Brook brought prosperity to St. Helens and Warrington.

But there was much opposition to each of these undertakings, from landowners who objected to the diversion of the streams, from traders of old-established river ports like York, Gainsborough, and Bawtry, and from all who disliked the idea of paying tolls on what had been thought of as free waterways. At their best, English rivers could provide but a slow and expensive means of transport. The use of them, no longer as highways, but as feeders for a more efficient system of canals, was among the most important of the innovations of the later decades of the century.

Internal trade was conducted by merchants most of whom specialized in a narrow range of products. Some themselves travelled about the country, but many employed 'riders-out' to secure orders and collect payment from customers. In overseas trade the merchant was a specialist, not in a particular commodity, but in a particular market. He had long ceased to voyage with his wares, which were now entrusted to a supercargo or dispatched to an agent abroad. Though ships were relatively small, the costs of construction, equipment, and repair were too great to be borne by a single person: many merchants, manufacturers, master mariners, and others held a fourth, a sixteenth, a thirty-second, or even a sixty-fourth share in what was in effect a joint-stock enterprise; and in this way a large part of the well-to-do came to take an active interest in coastwise and foreign trade.

Britain was self-supporting in foodstuffs and, on balance, was an exporter of grain. But she leaned heavily on foreign countries for timber, bar iron, hemp and other materials needed for the building and maintenance of her ships; for silk, cotton, and dyestuffs used in the textile industries; and for sugar, rum, tea, coffee, and tobacco, as well as for many finished products. In return Britain exported manufactured goods of all kinds, but especially those made of wool, iron, and leather. Cloth, firearms, hardware, and trinkets were sent to Africa and exchanged for slaves, who were shipped to the West Indies to pay for the luxuries and raw material which constituted the final cargo in this disreputable, triangular trade.

Historians have tended to pay undue attention to the commerce with distant lands. The overwhelming bulk of the import and export trade was with the Continent and, in particular, with the countries nearest to Britain. Compared with this, the traffic with India, the West Indies, and North America was small, and that with Africa insignificant. The fortunes made by members of the East India and Africa Companies must not be allowed to hide the fact that it was not the monopolistic organizations, trafficking in gold and slaves, but individual merchants—of London, the out-ports, and scores of inland towns—dealing in wares of common use, that built up British commerce at this time. Trade with the Baltic, from which Britain drew her naval stores, was of more political and economic consequence than that with the whole of the tropics.

II

In this highly condensed account of the chief activities that were to figure in the industrial revolution there are many omissions. Lack of space (and in some cases lack of knowledge) precludes a description of the builders and shipwrights, fishermen and sailors, tanners and leathermakers, papermakers and printers, and many others. It is unlikely, however, that a study of these would modify in any important respect the outline of the picture that has been presented.

Industry was rural rather than urban. In the two preceding centuries it had moved away from the towns to the countryside, partly to escape from municipal and gild restrictions, partly for technical reasons. Dependence on the sea for the carriage of goods led to a greater peopling of the coastal, than of the inland, regions; and the importance of transport by river was reflected in a thickening of population along the valleys of the Thames, Severn, and Clyde. There was concentration on the flanks of the Pennines, the Cotswolds, the Devonshire moors, and the uplands of southern Scotland, all of which were sources, not only of wool, but of the soft water needed for several of the processes of what was still the staple British industry. Corn mills, fulling mills, furnaces, forges, slitting mills, and cutlery and tool-grinding works depended on falling water for their power. Few towns (Sheffield was one of the few) had supplies of water sufficient to maintain many such plants, and in any case the ironworks needed to be near the woodlands, and the metal trades to the coal mines, which provided the fuel. The distribution of natural resources, and especially that of water, led to a wide geographical spread of population.

There were, it is true, towns of substantial size—sea-ports, river ports, and marketing centres. London, with its shipyards, warehouses, breweries and distilleries, and its varied crafts producing consumers' goods (silks and leather-ware, furniture, clocks and watches, glass, pottery, cutlery and jewellery) occupied an even more important place in the economic life of the nation than it does to-day. But it owed this development to its position as a capital city and a port; and the aggregation of population in London and the neighbouring parts of Middlesex, Surrey, and Kent was originally less the result of manufacture than of trade—as was also that of other large towns, like Bristol, Norwich, and Glasgow.

Industries were migratory (which is not to say that the workers and entrepreneurs themselves migrated). Iron production was transferred from the Weald to the West Midlands, silk and hosiery from London to East Anglia, the Midlands and the North; and salt-making from the coast of Durham to the plains of Cheshire. The structure of industry was flexible. The textile, clothing, hardware, and many other trades were carried on under what the text-books call the domestic system of industry —a phrase, convenient indeed, but misleading, for the chief characteristic of these trades is that they conformed to no single system of organization. Men of different degrees of skill, capital, and ability to bear risks could find in them full scope for their endowments, and there was a wide, almost a bewildering, variety of forms. The same was true, though in less degree, of mining and iron-making. Two or three partners, with very little capital, could open a pit or erect a forge, and compete, not unsuccessfully, with great enterprises like those of the Grand Allies of the Tyne or the Quaker dynasties of Shropshire.

Since processes were relatively simple men and women moved easily from one occupation to another: there was much coming and going between manufacture and agriculture; and mines, furnaces, and cottage workshops suspended their activities in the summer and early autumn so that the workers could help with the harvests. Most of the capital was embodied, not in buildings and machines, but in stocks of material in process of production: resources could be transferred readily from industry to trade, or from trade to industry; and a man might describe himself at one time as a master manufacturer and at another as a merchant. Since combinations of workers were few and weak, it was not difficult to substitute capital for labour, or one kind of labour for another; and the specialization of factors of production, which is the pre-requisite of a lowering of costs, could proceed with little or no restraint.

In such respects industry, in the period 1700–60, conformed closely to the models constructed by economists a century or more later. There is a danger, however, of overstressing the social advantages of the scheme of things, and, in particular, of idealizing the conditions of labour. It is doubtful whether the union of manufacture and agriculture was altogether a happy one for the worker, for it meant that his hands became roughened and gnarled in a way that confined his work—in textiles especially—to the coarser types of product. It is true that most workers enjoyed whatever advantages may be supposed to attach to ownership of their tools and appliances. But the acquisition of a pick and shovel, an anvil and hammer, or a set of saws and files was almost always the occasion of a debt. There could be little comfort in a cottage in which the principal piece of furniture was a loom or a knitting frame, and in which the atmosphere was heavy with fluff and dust, or with fumes from the charcoal stoves used in wool-combing and many other operations. It is true, again, that most workers were free in some measure to determine their hours of work and play. In mining absenteeism seems to have been at least as common as it is to-day, and holidays were numerous and well observed. Many domestic workers were accustomed to give Sunday, Monday, and sometimes Tuesday, to idleness or sport. This meant, however, that they had to work long into the night for the rest of the week; and though the irregularity was not, perhaps, of much consequence for the adult (some writers of books behave in much the same way) it can hardly have been good for the children who helped him.

Relations between employers and workers are generally best when they are direct. In agriculture many labourers were servants who lived in, though there was a growing tendency for them to set up homes of their own. But in industries in which the workers were scattered over a wide area, and in which (as in the manufacture of cotton and wool) a man might give employment to 2,000 or 3,000 people, personal contact was impossible. The closest ties were those among members of the group who worked together: in mining and fishing the 'company', in glass-making the 'chair', and in most cases the family. But the fact that men, women and children worked side by side does not imply that the household was a self-contained unit: no woman could spin the quantity (or variety) of yarn that her husband required, for technique was such that the full-time work of five or six spinners was needed to keep a single loom in operation. The intermediary saved the weaver from having to go to and fro in search of yarn, but he tended to drive hard bargains: in the Midlands the master-stockinger was rarely regarded as a friend; and in Lancashire when people heard a story of distress they sometimes said, 'It 'ud melt th' heart of a whetstone, or what's harder a putter-eaut.'

Except in agriculture most of the workers were paid by the piece. In many industries it was usual for them to receive a round sum weekly or fortnightly to cover subsistence, and the balance of their earnings (if any) at the end of a period of six, eight, or twelve weeks. In the Midlands and South Wales the miners were engaged, not only to hew and draw the coal, but also to deliver it to the customer: they were entitled to payment only when it had been sold, and a delay in transport or the closing of a market might mean that they were deprived of their earnings for many weeks or even months. Such an arrangement threw the risks of production on to the shoulders of those least able to bear them; and, in all industries in which the 'long pay' existed, the workers tended to spend freely, even lavishly, for a few days after the pay, and to live for the rest of their time at a level of comfort far below that which a more rational distribution of resources would have afforded. It was not until after the industrial revolution, when the employers assumed fully the function of providing capital and bearing risks, that regularity of wage payment and, with it, regularity of expenditure were attained.

Many workers received their earnings, not from their employer or his agent, but from a superior workman. This was so in those areas of coal-mining in which the butty system prevailed; it was so in the east of Scotland where the woman 'fremd' bearer was bound to the hagger or collier and received her pittance from him, and to some extent in Northumberland and Durham where the pitmen employed and paid the 'foals' or 'colts', who were often their own children. In many of the metal trades, in pin-making, and in the varied crafts of London, production was carried on by outworkers who employed other journeymen; and even in the highly organized establishment of Ambrose Crowley the smiths, following the custom of the trade, paid their own hammermen. The London silk-weavers hired women to wind, and children to fill the quills for their shuttles. Almost everywhere there was a degraded form of apprenticeship, of both boys and girls, which offered little or no training; and many children suffered from hunger, over-work, and ill-treatment. It was not in industries like iron-smelting, where large-scale capital and well-to-do employers ruled, but in the poorly developed domestic trades, that the conditions of labour were at their worst.

The more highly skilled workers in agriculture, and in the coal, iron, pottery, and other trades, were hired for long periods, usually for the year. The bonds under which they served gave them some security of employment and, incidentally, were a safeguard against impressment into the Forces of the Crown—a body of poor repute which only the destitute would join of their own free will. But the price of security was the loss of freedom to move. The Scottish colliers and salt-workers were guaranteed subsistence, but they were bound, by custom and law, to work at the same place and the same job for life. And even in England, where such conditions of serfdom had long been swept away, it was a question whether the lot of the skilled worker was more eligible than that of the labourer or semi-skilled weaver, who, if he was often without employment, might change his occupation, and (within the limits of the laws of settlement) his place of work, at will.

There were many sources of industrial disharmony, especially in the domestic trades. Some employers used false weights in giving out yarn or iron, and demanded from the workers more cloth or nails than the material would run to. Others gave out faulty raw material or were irregular in their payments. In the more remote areas, where there were few retail shops, and where the supply of money was inadequate, truck was common. On the other hand, the spinners, weavers, knitters, nailmakers, and so on were often unpunctual in returning their work; textile workers mixed butter and grease with the fabric to increase the weight, and nailmakers substituted inferior iron for the rods they had received from the warehouse. Filching of material was widespread. Acts of Parliament, with increasingly heavy penalties, were passed in 1703, 1740, 1749, and 1777, in an attempt to check it; and in the last of these years the employers were given the power to enter shops or outhouses for the purpose of search. At this time the first of a number of Worsted Committees was set up to deal with embezzlement and delays in the return of work. The inspectors appointed by them were licensed by the Justices and formed what was, in effect, an industrial police. In the wide areas in which they operated the workers were subject to a discipline little less complete than that of the factory-master, without the compensation in regularity of employment and hours that the factory was to offer.

The organization of production through a series of merchants and intermediaries necessitated a system of credit. But the obverse of credit is debt. The domestic workers were often debtors to their employers, not only for material, but also for sums of money borrowed to meet the emergencies of birth, sickness, death, or removal to a new home. The claims of the lender were met by deductions from future earnings, and sometimes children were set to work for the employer without wages, as a means of settlement. Often before one obligation was met a new one was incurred: wages books afford many instances of workers who were never free from debt. Goods were bought from pedlars on credit, ale scores were run up at the tavern, and when payment was demanded, a new call was made on the employer. In many towns special courts were set up for the recovery of small debts, as well as to deal with the theft of material. Indebtedness—especially indebtedness to an employer—must have weakened, not only the morals, but also the bargaining power of men and women who, at the best, were never in a position to argue effectively about wages.

There was a tendency for employers to spread work lightly over a large number of workers, partly to ensure that they would not be short of labour in times of pressure. The hosiers and stockingers had a special incentive to do this, for the more knitters they employed the greater their income from frame-rents. The skill needed for most domestic occupations was easily acquired, and the opportunity of employment for all members of the family acted as a magnet. As with industries that make use of casual labour to-day, more people entered these trades than could be assured of regular work. Under-employment, rather that periodic unemployment, was the bane of the domestic worker.

There are writers who assert that the existence of a

supply of labour in excess of the demand is the result of 'the exhaustion of investment opportunities' which is said to be a feature of 'a late stage of capitalism'. But, in the period 1700–60, before capitalism had come to maturity or opportunities of investment were fully open, large numbers of people had no regular means of employment. The beggars and vagrants, thieves and highwaymen, prostitutes and parasites of various kinds formed a much larger section of the population than to-day. But, these apart, there was a substantial body of men and women, on the fringe of the economic system, who eked out a living by honest means if they could—the squatters on the waste and the semi-employed cottagers and garret-dwellers of the towns. These formed a large part of that mass of the 'poor' whose untidy and imprudent manner of living was an affront to the reason and good sense of early economists like Dean Tucker. Some of them, indeed, were poor because of defects of character, but others because, at the prevailing level of investment, there was little or no work for them to do. It was not the least of the achievements of the industrial revolution that it drew into the economic system part of that legion of the lost, and that it turned many of the irregulars into efficient, if over-regimented, members of an industrial army.

To the question why the industrial revolution did not come earlier many answers can be given. In the first half of the eighteenth century there was much ingenuity and contrivance, but time was needed for this to reach fruition. Some of the early inventions failed because of incomplete thought, others because the right material was not to hand, because of lack of skill or adaptability

on the part of the workers, or because of social resistance
to change. Industry had to await the coming of capital
in quantities large enough, and at a price low enough,
to make it possible to construct large buildings and appliances. It had to wait until the idea of progress—as an
ideal and as a process at work in society—spread from
the minds of the few to those of the many. But, such
large considerations apart, in each of the major industries there was some obstacle—some bottle-neck, to use
the current phrase—which had to be removed before expansion could go far. In agriculture it was the common
rights and the lack of winter fodder; in mining the want
of an efficient device to deal with flood water; in iron-
making the shortage of suitable fuel; in the metal
trades a consequent shortage of material; and in textiles
an inadequate supply of yarn. Transport, trade, and
credit alike suffered from the dead hand of monopolistic
organization, and the arrested development of these services had adverse effects on industry in general. Thus
it was that, though there was growth in every field of
human endeavour, change was never so rapid as to
endanger the stability of existing institutions. In the
period 1700–60 Britain experienced no revolution, either
in the technique of production, the structure of industry,
or the economic and social life of the people.

E

CHAPTER III

THE TECHNICAL INNOVATIONS

'ABOUT 1760 a wave of gadgets swept over England.' So, not inaptly, a schoolboy began his answer to a question on the industrial revolution. It was not only gadgets, however, but innovations of various kinds—in agriculture, transport, manufacture, trade, and finance—that surged up with a suddenness for which it is difficult to find a parallel at any other time or place. The quickened pace of development is attested by the catalogue of new patents, the lengthening list of Acts of enclosure, the expanding figures of output and exports, and the course of prices, which, after remaining roughly steady for two generations, now began an ascent that was to continue for more than half a century. The story of a period the opening decade of which alone saw the innovations associated with the names of Brindley, Roebuck, Wedgwood, Hargreaves, Arkwright, and Watt can hardly be told in terms of an evolutionary process.

It has already been suggested that this period of time was propitious for invention and expansion. The fall in the rate of interest, coinciding as it did with an expansion of markets at home and abroad, provided the incentive. Pelham's conversion of the Debt from $3\frac{1}{2}$ to 3 per cent. had been completed in 1757; and although the Seven Years War pressed down the price of Consols, and closed some doors to British trade, the return of peace in 1763 brought with it a rate for public borrowing which did not exceed $3\frac{3}{4}$ per cent., and an opening of new areas to enterprise and capital in the Far East and West alike. At the same time the barriers imposed by the shortages of food, fuel, iron, yarn, and transport were being thrown down at a speed which makes it difficult to determine where the priority lay. And just as an obstacle in the path of any one industry had led to congestion in that of others, so now its removal produced a widespread liberation. Innovation is a process which, once under way, tends to accelerate.

In agriculture enclosure went on apace. It spread from parishes where the occupiers were few to those where they were many; and, since there was hostility, it was necessary to proceed by Act of Parliament instead of by deed of mutual agreement. A petition signed by the owners of four-fifths of the land (but usually by a much smaller proportion of the number of owners) was sent to Westminster; and in due course a Bill was passed 'for dividing, allotting, and enclosing the open and common fields, meadows, pastures, and common and waste lands' of the particular parish. In the ten years beginning in 1740 there had been thirty-eight such Acts, and in the following ten years 156. But in the decade that opened in 1760 there were no fewer than 480, and much higher figures than this were to follow. The initiative usually came from the squire and the tithe-owner. A Parliament in which the landed interest was supreme paid little heed to protests. And, though the commissioners appointed under each separate Act seem to have been scrupulous in dealing with those who could establish a legal right to the land, they generally ignored the equitable claims of those whose only title was that they, and perhaps their forefathers, had tilled the soil, until now without challenge. The story of enclosures, indeed, fits well into the scheme of those who write economic history in terms of a class struggle, with the rich exerting political and economic power to impose their will on the poor. But the full story must also take account of a concerted effort to increase the productivity of the soil at a time when wars and bad harvests were threatening the existence of a growing urban society. There were many disreputable incidents associated with enclosure, but it is not enough to treat the whole movement as though it were just a smash-and-grab raid by a gang of aristocratic adventurers.

The open-field village was not wholly stagnant. In some places new rotations, which included a crop of clover, had been introduced; but an Act of 1773, which sought to encourage such improvements by allowing the farmers to elect field-reeves, proved abortive. To close observers like Arthur Young the system appeared as a moribund survival of subsistence farming that must be swept away if England was to survive. In 1801—a year of war and also a year of famine—the General Enclosure Act simplified procedure and reduced costs, and from this time to 1815 the movement proceeded rapidly.

Not long ago it was generally believed that the enclosures were responsible for the decline of the yeoman freeholder, for a replacement of small estates by large, and for an extensive rural depopulation. It is true that there were fewer yeomen at the end of the eighteenth century than in earlier times; but recent statistical inquiries show that the freeholders had largely been bought out long before the period of Parliamentary enclosures. (After 1780, indeed, occupying ownership seems to have increased, for, as in 1914–20, many farmers made use of their wartime profits to purchase

heir holdings.) It is true that the larger farms tended to
become bigger; but the number small enough to be
worked by a single family also increased. It is true, once
again, that where the enclosed land was turned to
pasture less labour was required, and many cottars
and squatters were bought out, or turned off. But,
during the wars, when the urgent need was for more
grain, the arable area, which required much labour,
was expanding. Increasingly as time went on it was the
waste that was the subject of enclosure, and the bringing
into cultivation of land that had previously hardly been
worked at all must have increased employment. Some
agricultural workers, there is no doubt, migrated to
nearby towns; but that they were attracted to manufacture, rather than repelled from agriculture, is indicated
by the relatively high level of farm wages in the neighbourhood of the industrial centres. The fact that no
single county of England registered a decline of population between 1801 and 1851 suggests that there was no
widespread depeopling of the countryside at this time.

The technical developments of the period were not,
indeed, of a labour-saving kind. Farming offers relatively
little scope for specialization, and extensive use of
machinery on the land came only with the twentieth
century. In the 1780s new types of ploughs were introduced, and a Scottish millwright devised a more efficient
threshing machine. The increased output of iron led to
a substitution of metal for wood in the frame of the
plough, as well as in parts of the harrow and the roller;
and in 1803 a ploughshare of steel was put on the
market. None of these innovations, however, was of
consequence: it is in other directions that we must look
for the major changes in agricultural technique.

In 1760, Joseph Elkington began to develop new methods of drainage in Warwickshire. About the same time Robert Bakewell (1725–94) of Dishley in Leicestershire, using empirical methods of inbreeding, was producing cattle which gave a bigger yield of beef, as well as horses of greater power, and sheep of larger size and weight. From the late 'seventies Coke of Holkham (1752–1842) was expending vast sums on the improvement of his estate, making use of marls and clover, introducing new grasses and artificial feeds, giving inducements to tenants to keep their land in good heart, and advertising widely the merits of Norfolk husbandry. Other aristocrats, and George III himself, took up with enthusiasm the cause of agricultural improvement. Knowledge of new methods was spread at tenants' dinners, shearing feasts, and the more frequent meetings of many local farmers' clubs. The Society of Arts offered prizes for new devices, and the institution of county and regional agricultural societies aided the process. In 1776 there appeared the first number of the *Farmers' Magazine*, and in 1806 that of the *Farmers' Journal*. Treatises on agricultural methods, and publications like those in which Arthur Young described his rides through England, Ireland, France, Italy, and Spain, helped to break down the isolation and parochialism of rural life. And in 1793 Sir John Sinclair (1745–1835) set up, with some support from Government, a voluntary society known as the Board of Agriculture, the reports of which have much to say of the experiments that were being made by obscure farmers in many parts of the country. There is, however, a danger of assuming that the improvements made by enlightened landlords and progressive cultivators were typical. The Norfolk rotation, the improved methods of breeding, the Rotherham plough, the substitution of the horse for the ox, and of wheat for rye or oats, were innovations that spread slowly. It was only in the East and East Midland counties that progress was marked, and in many parts of the country farming was carried on very much as it had been centuries before.

Production for the market, together with improved transport, encouraged a growth of geographical specialization and of trade between one region and another. The eastern and southern areas gave primacy to grain, the Midlands to cattle and horses, and the Home Counties to dairy produce and vegetables. Cattle were brought from Scotland to East Anglia, and from Wales to Essex, to be fattened for the market. Lambs were sent from Wiltshire to Middlesex, and from Nottingham to Worcester, and ewes for breeding came back in exchange. There were many minor specialisms—Cheshire cheese, Norfolk turkeys, Aylesbury ducks, Kent hops, and Hampshire honey. But the technical advantages of mixed farming were so great that the concentration was rarely, if ever, absolute.

Custom came to play a smaller, and competition a larger, part in the determination of rents and wages. There was a rise in the standard of life of the labourers, at least in the North, though the decline of rural crafts pressed hard on many family budgets. But the workers had less security than in the past: with the improvements in threshing of the 1820s, there was less occupation on farms in the winter months, and the agricultural labourer began to share with the townsman the experience of technological unemployment. To the townsman himself, the progress of farming brought little but gain.

Wheat came to take the place of rye and barley as the staple foods in the Midlands, and of oatmeal in the North and Scotland. Potatoes were brought into general use, and meat was no longer a luxury. A better and more varied diet was not without effect on the health and expectation of life of the workers, nor was it least among the causes of expansion of industrial output.

Like agriculture, the mining of coal offered little scope for the application of machinery or sudden changes in technique. Here, as in all extractive industries, progress was by small increments. The introduction of ponies into the pits of the North, about the middle of the century, greatly reduced the cost of coal, for it meant that the barrowmen, who had formed the majority of the underground workers, could now be replaced by boys, whose wages were relatively low. The increased output of iron, itself based on coal, had important effects on mining practice. The use of cast-iron tubbing in the shaft made it possible to sink to greater depths; and the cast-iron rail, which John Curr introduced into the pits about Sheffield in 1777, effected a further economy in underground transport. The wheeled corf which he devised to run on the rails could be brought up the shaft without being unloaded at the pit bottom, and this again meant a lowering of costs. Methods of ventilation were improved when, in the 'sixties, Carlisle Spedding of White-haven introduced the use of brattices to guide the air through the underground ways, and still more, in the 'nineties, when John Buddle brought into the Northumberland field his system of triple shafts and more elaborate methods of 'coursing'. The process of hewing the coal remained much as before, but the supporting pillars of coal were 'robbed' until they became slender columns; and towards the end of the century gunpowder came into use for blasting the rock. Illumination continued to present a major problem until, in 1813–15, Sir Humphry Davy, Dr. Clanny, and George Stephenson produced their several safety lamps, the first application of which brought, it is said, not greater security of life to the miner, but a larger output of coal—from seams that had previously been considered too dangerous to be worked at all.

In the iron industry the coke-fed blast furnaces had been growing steadily in size and number, and new areas of enterprise had been opened up. Stimulated by the demand for munitions, many new works, including those of John Wilkinson at Broseley and of John Roebuck at Carron, were set up during the war of 1756–63. In its magnitude and the variety of its products (which included the famous carronades) the Carron ironworks was a portent of a new type of undertaking; and the lighting of its first furnace, on 1 January 1760, may serve to mark, for those who like to be precise in such matters, the beginning of the industrial revolution in Scotland.

Though charcoal had still to be used in converting the coke-smelted pig into bar iron, mineral fuel was increasingly employed in the early stages of this process; and the brothers Cranage, who were employees of the Coalbrookdale Company, came near to success in their attempt to use coke alone for the purpose in 1766. It was not, however, until 1783–4 that a final solution was reached, when Henry Cort (1740–1800), a Navy agent who had set up a forge near Fareham, took out his two patents or puddling and rolling. Cort's method was first to re-heat the pig iron with coke until it was in a pasty form, then to stir it with iron rods until much of the carbon and impurities had been burnt away, and finally to pass it between iron rollers which pressed out the dross that remained. His discovery was one of the outstanding events in the history of technology. It had the effect of freeing the forge-masters from their dependence on the woodlands, just as Darby's discovery had freed the furnace owners. It liberated Britain from the necessity of importing large amounts of charcoal-iron from the Baltic, at a time when political relations with Sweden and Russia were liable to rupture. It drew the forge branch of the industry from its scattered haunts to the coalfields, where the making of finished iron could be carried on in close proximity to the furnaces. And it led to the growth of great integrated establishments, in which all processes, from the mining of ore and coal to the slitting of rods, were controlled by a single group of proprietors. Within a relatively short space of time the industry came to be concentrated in four main areas, and new types of communities, with dense populations, grew up around the pithills and slagheaps of Staffordshire, South Yorkshire, the Clyde, and South Wales. The output of iron increased vastly; metal came to take the place of timber and stone in works of construction; the hardware industries expanded the range of their products; and there was hardly an activity—from agriculture to ship-building, from engineering to weaving —that did not experience the animating effects of cheap iron.

A generation or so later came the discovery by David Mushet of the black-band ironstone in Scotland, and close on the heels of this the introduction by J. B.

Neilson of the hot-blast, which resulted in a further increase in the output of the furnace. The dates of these inventions fall within the bounds of our period, but it was not until the 'thirties and 'forties that their full effects were felt.

Cort's invention of puddling and rolling, like many other technical inventions of the time, could not have been effective without the aid of a new form of power. Until the sixties of the eighteenth century Newcomen's engine remained a contrivance for the useful but limited purpose of pumping water. It is true that the water, raised to a height, could be used to drive a wheel and so to work machines of various kinds; but the expenditure of energy involved in the process was great —so great that a Scot, at any rate, could not bear to see it. At the University of Glasgow, Joseph Black (1728–99) was delivering lectures on the phenomenon (which he had discovered) of latent heat, and John Anderson was making use, in his class on Natural Philosophy, of a model of the engine. Not himself a member of the University, but a mathematical instrument-maker whose shop was within the precincts, James Watt (1736–1819) was called upon to repair the model. He saw that the chief defect of the atmospheric engine arose from the alternate injection and condensation of steam: in order to prevent the steam from condensing before the piston had completed its upward stroke, it was necessary to keep the cylinder warm; but, equally, in order to condense the steam for the return stroke, it was necessary for it to be cold. The sudden changes in the temperature of the cylinder wall meant that a great amount of potential energy ran to waste.

Watt had had many conversations with Black, Anderson, John Robison, and other members of the University about these things, and had pondered deeply on them for many months. Then, by a sudden flash of inspiration which came, in 1765, in the course of a Sunday-afternoon stroll across the Green, he hit on the solution of introducing a separate condenser which could be kept permanently cool while the cylinder could be kept permanently hot. Within a few weeks a model was made, but many years were to pass before the technical difficulties of translating this into a full-scale engine were overcome. Watt's experiments were financed by John Roebuck, who held a share in the patent which was taken out in 1769. But the Carron ironworks could not supply the skilled artisans whose help was essential, and most of Watt's own energies had to be given to earning a living by work as a surveyor and civil engineer. In 1774, however, Roebuck, whose affairs had become embarrassed, transferred his share in the patent to Matthew Boulton (1728–1809), and James Watt left Scotland for Birmingham. Here he had the support of a man, already well established in business, endowed with a sanguine temperament, and driven by an ambition which extended far beyond that of merely making money.

At Boulton's Soho works there were the craftsmen Watt needed to make the valves and other delicate parts of the engine. Not far away was the Coalbrook-dale ironworks, with its long experience of producing castings for the atmospheric engine, and near at hand, at Bradley, was the great ironmaster, John Wilkinson (1728–1808), whose patent, of 1774, for boring cannon could be adapted to boring cylinders with an accuracy that had not hitherto been attained. Watt was fortunate in his associates. The researches of Black, who laid down the first principles, the capital and enterprise of Boulton, the ingenuity of Wilkinson, the technical skill of Murdoch, Southern, and a host of obscure artificers, were all necessary to the making of the steam engine. It was Watt's merit, not only that he was among the first to apply to industry the methods of systematic experiment used in pure science, but that he was able to synthesize the ideas of others and bring together the varied skills required for the creation of a complex mechanism.

In 1775 Parliament extended Watt's patent for a further quarter of a century to 1800. During the first six years of this period the engine remained a single-acting device for producing a reciprocating stroke. It had an efficiency four times that of the atmospheric engine, and was used extensively for pumping water at reservoirs, brine works, breweries, and distilleries, and in the metal mines of Cornwall. In the coal industry, however, it played a relatively small part. For Watt based his premiums on the difference between the fuel consumption of the Newcomen engine and that of his own; and since, at the collieries, economy of small coal was of no consequence, there was little incentive to substitute new engines for old. In the iron industry, on the other hand, the contrivance was used to raise water to turn the great wheels which operated the bellows, forge hammers, and rolling mills; and, even at this first stage of development, it had important effects on output.

If Watt had done no more than this he would have established a claim to a place in the front rank of British inventors. But he could not rest satisfied with having made improvements, however great, in what was little more than a steam pump. His mind had long been busy with the idea of converting the to-and-fro action into a rotary movement, capable of turning machinery, and this was made possible by a number of devices, including the sun-and-planet, a patent for which was taken out in 1781. In the following year came the double-acting, rotative engine, in which the expansive force of steam was applied to both sides of the piston; in 1784 the parallel motion; and in 1788 the beautiful device of the governor, which gave the greater regularity and smoothness of working essential in a prime mover for the more delicate and intricate of industrial processes.

The introduction of the rotative engine was a momentous event. Coinciding in time as it did with that of Cort's puddling and rolling of iron, and following closely on the inventions of Arkwright and Crompton, it completely transformed the conditions of life of hundreds of thousands of men and women. After 1783, when the first of the new engines was erected—to work a hammer for John Wilkinson at Bradley—it became clear that a technological revolution was afoot in Britain. Before their patents expired in 1800, Boulton and Watt had built and put into operation about 500 engines, of both types, at home and (in a few instances) abroad. The new form of power and, no less, the new transmitting mechanisms by which this was made to do work previously done by hand and muscle, were the pivot on which industry swung into the modern age.

It was in the manufacture of textiles that the transformation was most rapid. Already, important changes had come about in spinning, and the problem of the shortage of yarn, which had for so long held back the development of weaving, had been solved. Sometime between 1764 and 1767, James Hargreaves, a weaver-carpenter of Blackburn, had devised a simple hand machine, called the jenny, by means of which a woman could spin, at first six or seven, but later as many as eighty, threads at once. Unfortunately for him, he made and sold a number of jennies before he took out a patent in 1770, and for this reason it was later held in the courts that his claim was invalid. The jenny was adopted with enthusiasm, first in Nottingham, and afterwards in Lancashire; and by 1788 there were, it is estimated, about 20,000 of the machines at work in England. The jenny was small enough to be housed in a cottage; it was cheap to construct; and no great strength was needed to operate it. Hence it fitted well into the existing framework of domestic industry; and, since the spinner was now able to keep pace with the weaver, the effect was to strengthen, rather than weaken, the family economy. The jenny-spun yarn, however, was soft, and suitable therefore only for weft: the warp had still to be spun on the hand-wheel, until, following close on the invention of Hargreaves, came that connected with the name of Arkwright.

Richard Arkwright (1732–92) was a barber and wig-maker of Preston. Not himself, it would seem, of any great inventive ability, he had the force of character and robust sense that are traditionally associated with his native county—with little, it may be added, of the kindliness and humour that are, in fact, the dominant traits of Lancashire people. Helped by a Warrington clockmaker, John Kay (who had assisted Thomas Highs of Leigh in experiments in spinning), he produced, in 1768, the 'frame', a patent for which was granted to him in the following year. In appearance the frame was similar to the contrivance of Lewis Paul—it made use of rollers to draw out the rovings before these passed to the spindle— though whether or not Arkwright, Kay, or Highs had actually seen a machine of Paul's construction must remain in doubt. The product was a strong, if somewhat coarse, twist, suitable for warps, and less expensive than the linen that had generally been used for the purpose. It was on the basis of cheap calicoes, made entirely of cotton, that the first stage of the industrial revolution in textiles was built.

Like Hargreaves, Arkwright soon left Lancashire for Nottingham where the demand of the hosiers offered an immediate market for his yarn. Unlike the jenny, the frame required, for its working, power greater than that of human muscles, and hence from the beginning the process was carried on in mills or factories. After experiments in small establishments in which the power was provided by horses, Arkwright sought the support of the well-to-do hosiers, Samuel Need of Nottingham and Jedediah Strutt of Derby. In 1771 he set up a large water-driven factory at Cromford—modelled, it is said, on Lombe's silk works at Derby—where within a very short time he was giving employment to about 600 workers, most of them children. It soon became apparent that the older methods of carding were no longer able to supply material in quantities sufficient to meet the needs of the spinners; and in 1775, drawing together the ideas of others, and adding to these the crank and comb, Arkwright obtained a patent for card- ing by cylinders. This, like spinning by rollers, required extra-human power, and henceforth it was usual for the two processes to be carried on, side by side, in the factory. New mills were set up at Belper and Milford in Derbyshire, and in 1777 the first of the water-driven factories in Lancashire was erected near Chorley. After 1781 when the Manchester cotton spinners (determined opponents of all forms of monopoly as they were) succeeded in getting the carding patent revoked, hundreds of workmen were busy running up new factories in the countryside, not only of Lancashire but also of Cheshire, Derbyshire, Nottinghamshire, Yorkshire, and North Wales.

About the middle of the 'eighties the situation was again changed by yet another innovation in spinning. After seven years of experiment in his 'conjuring room' at Hall-i'-th'-Wood, a Bolton weaver, Samuel Crompton (1753–1827), succeeded in producing a yarn, at once strong, fine and even, suitable for both warp and weft, and adapted to the making of all kinds of textiles, but especially to that of the fine muslins which had hitherto been imported as a luxury from the East. The machine had features of both the jenny and the water-frame and, because of its supposed cross-bred origin, came to be known as the mule. Probably because the wide terms of Arkwright's specification barred the way, no patent was taken out. And when, in 1785, both of Arkwright's patents were finally cancelled, the field for enterprise was open to all. In the same year Watt's steam engine was first applied to spinning by rollers, and, after 1790, when steam power was used to drive the mules, it became possible to put up large factories in towns. This did not mean, however, that the country factories declined: on the contrary, their numbers increased steadily until about the end of the first decade of the new century— partly because the machines driven by water were

F

subject to less vibration, and were therefore better for spinning fine counts, than those driven by steam. But the growth of the urban factories was rapid: whereas in 1782 there had been only two cotton mills in and about Manchester, in 1802 the number had reached fifty-two; and by 1811 four-fifths of the cotton goods produced in Lancashire were made of mule yarn, most of it spun in the towns.

In the late 'eighties and early 'nineties the demand for the new muslins was so great that the weavers of these (though not the weavers of coarser cloths) experienced high prosperity. There was, indeed, a boom, and large numbers of men and women were drawn into the weaving branch of the industry. This was the period which saw a rapid conversion of barns and brewhouses into weaving sheds, and the throwing up of 'loom houses', attached to cottages, all over the countryside. But the 'golden age of the weavers' was not destined to last. Already in 1784, a clergyman-poet, Edmund Cartwright, foreseeing the developments that would follow the end of Arkwright's patents, had devised a power-loom which could be operated by horses, water-wheels, or steam engines. Unlike the devices for spinning, the power-loom made relatively slow progress: many improvements had to be brought about in the loom before it could be an effective instrument of factory production. New contrivances for dressing the warp and taking up the cloth on the beam were introduced by William Radcliffe and Thomas Johnson in 1803 and 1804; and further developments were made in the following decade by Horrocks of Stockport and Roberts of Manchester. But even in 1813 it was estimated that there were not more than 2,400 power-looms in the country, as against nearly a hundred times that number of looms operated by hand. After the end of the French war the pace of development quickened: by 1820 there were about 14,000, and by 1833 about 100,000 power-looms in Britain. The attempt of the hand-loom weavers to compete with steam and the superior organization of the factory forms the subject of one of the most depressing chapters in the economic history of the period.

In many cases weaving was carried on by independent employers who specialized in this branch of the industry; but after 1820 a tendency developed for spinners to attach weaving sheds to their mills. As in the manufacture of iron, so in that of cotton, industrial change was associated with the rise of large concerns and integration of processes.

Most of the innovations in spinning and weaving cotton were applicable to the manufacture of other textile fabrics. But technological progress was, in fact, far less rapid in the woollen and worsted than in the cotton industry: even in the middle of the nineteenth century not more than half the Yorkshire textile workers, and still less of those of the West Country, had been brought into factories. The reason for this does not lie (as some have supposed) in innate conservatism: Yorkshiremen were then, as now, as alert and energetic as Lancastrians. It lay partly in the nature of the raw material; partly in the regulations which well-intentioned, but ill-informed, governments had made for the conduct of the industry; and partly in the fact that the demand for woollen cloths, at home and abroad, was less elastic than that for calicoes and muslins. Here and there large factories were set up by enterprising merchants like Benjamin Gott. But the typical business was a relatively small concern, owned by several men, who were associated as equals in what was, in effect, a joint-stock company. A few not inconsiderable fortunes were made in the West Riding, but there was no Arkwright or Peel, no woollen king to vie with the cotton kings to the west of the Pennines.

The later processes in the manufacture of cotton underwent changes hardly less great than those in carding, spinning and weaving. In the early years of the eighteenth century the printing of calicoes had been done by craftsmen who, making use of wooden blocks, impressed the pattern on the cloth by hand. The first innovation was the substitution of plates of copper; but the greatest step forward was made in 1783, when a Scot, Thomas Bell, replaced these by large revolving cylinders worked by power. His invention was at once adopted by the Peels and others in Lancashire, and the era of large-scale production in calico printing thus coincided almost precisely with that in carding and spinning. The other finishing processes of bleaching and dyeing were less susceptible of machine methods. But in these also a long series of innovations culminated, about the same time, in a revolution of technique and the growth of large-scale undertakings. The story is closely bound up with that of the discovery of new reagents and tinctures, largely by Scottish and French scientists, and with the rise of industrial chemistry in England.

The traditional method of bleaching was to expose the fabric to the rays of the sun, or to boil it, first in a solution of ashes and then in sour milk. The publication, in 1756, by an Edinburgh professor, Francis Home, of his *Art of Bleaching* pointed to the replacement of the sour milk by sulphuric acid, a material which was already in limited use for cleaning tinplate and other products of the metal trades. In 1736, an apothecary, Joshua Ward, had set up at Twickenham works in which, making use of an apparatus of glass, he was able to produce vitriol on a small scale. But the cost was great, and the real beginnings of industrial sulphuric acid came ten years or so later when John Roebuck, himself a trained chemist, joined with Samuel Garbett to establish works, first at Birmingham and later at Prestonpans, in which the acid was produced in vessels of lead. In 1787 Berthollet's process of bleaching by chlorine was brought from France by James Watt, and used by Watt's father-in-law, M'Gregor, and others in Scotland. And in 1798 Charles Tennant of Glasgow discovered a method of passing chlorine gas over slaked lime, and so of producing a bleaching powder, easier to handle and transport, and less injurious to health, than the liquid acids.

The production of bleaching materials was only one side of the application of chemistry to industry. Parallel to, and connected with, the manufacture of acids was that of alkalis and salts. At Prestonpans Roebuck had made use of vitriol and common salt to produce soda, and in 1773 James Keir (who had studied chemistry under Black and had served with Wolfe at Quebec) joined with another ex-serviceman, Alexander Blair, to set up works at Tipton. Here they made soda for the soapmakers, white lead for the potters, and litharge for the glassworks which they had themselves established earlier at Stourbridge. Other manufacturers engaged in the production of potash, alum and ammonia, a method of making the last of which had been discovered by

Priestley a few years earlier. At a later stage salt-water, coal, and supplies of sulphuric acid attracted the rising chemical industry to the area about the Tyne, where, early in the nineteenth century, the introduction by the Cooksons of the Leblanc process led to a rapid concentration of population about South Shields and Gateshead. But the greatest development came in the early 'twenties, when, encouraged by the reduction of the duties on salt, James Muspratt and Josiah Gamble left Ireland to exploit the Leblanc process at Liverpool. It was out of their concerns that there were to arise, later, the thriving, if unlovely, communities of St. Helens and Widnes.

Meanwhile, progress was being made with the derivatives of coal. As early as 1756 the Scottish geologist, James Hutton, had succeeded in extracting sal-ammoniac from soot. But it was yet another Scot, Alexander Cochrane, ninth Earl of Dundonald, who was responsible for the real exploitation of coal as a source of chemicals. Throughout the eighteenth century tar and pitch, essential for the protection of the timbers of vessels, were almost a monopoly of the Baltic Powers, which were thus in a position to exert diplomatic pressure on a nation increasingly dependent for its prosperity on shipping. Patriotism and self-interest, alike, led the Earl to experiment in extracting tar and varnish from the coals of his estate and, in 1782, to set up works for the purpose at Culross. Several circumstances favoured the enterprise. Joseph Black, Adam Smith, and a relative, J. L. Macadam, gave counsel; Parliament extended the patent to 1806; and the rapid expansion of coke-ovens, following on the inventions of Henry Cort, provided in their waste gases raw material in the form required.

But a shortage of capital, the conservatism of the Admiralty, and the temperament of Dundonald himself, led to financial loss. It was left to Macadam and his successors to reap the rewards of an innovation the potentialities of which have been fully realized only in our own day.

In the industries so far considered the growth of production was associated with new forms of power, new machinery or new knowledge derived from science. That these were not the only influences shaping the industrial revolution is evident from the development that took place in the manufacture of pottery. From the seventeenth century a growing shortage of tin and lead, and a growing taste for tea and coffee, had brought a gradual substitution of earthenware for metal in household utensils of various kinds. Porcelain from the East and Delft ware from Holland had appeared on the tables of the well-to-do, and cruder English pottery on those of the relatively poor. In the early part of the eighteenth century there were potteries at Lambeth, Chelsea, Bristol, Worcester, Liverpool and other urban centres; but the scarcity of wood fuel was driving the industry to the coalfields, and especially to north Staffordshire, where clays of various kinds and lead for glazing were close at hand. As in other trades producing consumers' goods, the works were small. The typical employer was a man who owned one or two sheds, a vat for mixing the clay with water, a sun-pan for evaporation, a single potter's wheel, worked by hand or foot, and an oven for baking the ware. The pots were sold to itinerant cratemen, who carried them away in panniers on the backs of donkeys. Progress was largely a matter of

developing new skills and of finding better clays, glazing
materials, and means of decoration. White clays from
Devon and Dorset, mixed with calcined flints, replaced
the coarser and duller clays of Staffordshire; salt was
brought from Cheshire for glazing (though by no means
to the exclusion of lead); cobalt came to be used for
tinting; and plaster of Paris was employed for making
the blocks or moulds in which the pottery was pressed or
cast. About the middle of the century the 'pyrometric
bead' was devised to measure the temperature of the
ovens, and a little later came the use of copper plates for
impressing designs on the ware.

In several of these developments a prominent part was
played by the family of the Wedgwoods, members of
which had been engaged in the industry from the early
years of the seventeenth century: it is with Josiah
Wedgwood (1730-95) that the growth of the Potteries
is most closely linked. In 1769 he set up near Hanley
the famous Etruria works which became, like Coalbrookdale, Cromford, and Soho, a model for many
other undertakings. Though not a trained scientist,
Wedgwood was tireless in experiment: he devised a
green glaze, introduced the cream-coloured pottery
known as Queen's ware, and perfected the jasper
(white figures in relief against a coloured background)
which comes to mind whenever the name of Wedgwood
is mentioned to-day. He had artistic sensibilities and
employed men of the quality of Flaxman and Webber to
design his 'ornamental' products; but he had also the
plain sense to know that his profits must come from the
manufacture on a large scale of what he called 'useful'
wares. A friend of Boulton and Watt, he took a keen
interest in the development of the steam-engine, and

made use of the new power for grinding materials and turning the lathes. But most of the work at Etruria was done by hand: it was by intensifying the division of labour that Wedgwood brought about the reduction of cost which enabled his pottery to find markets in all parts of Britain, and also in Europe and America. He built a village for his work-people, spent much money on the improvement of roads, and was Treasurer to the Grand Junction Canal, the opening of which, in 1777, brought a new era of prosperity to the Potteries, and to Etruria in particular. Though not the inventor of any one outstanding device, Wedgwood was an innovator of the first rank. He had the acumen to obtain a majority of the shares in the Cornish Clay Company, and his organizing abilities were shown, not only in the stress he laid on the training of labour, but also in the care he took in the selection of his salesmen and managers, and the attention he paid to the avoidance of waste. Beginning in humble circumstances, he died worth more than half a million, and in the process of making it he 'converted a rude and inconsiderable manufactory into an elegant art and an important element in national commerce'.

Among the new industries to which the eighteenth century gave rise perhaps the most important was engineering. It has been said that the civil engineer, as we know him to-day, is the lineal descendant of the military sapper of the wars of the seventeenth century. But, however it may have been in other parts of Europe, in England it was not strategic, but commercial, necessities that led to improvements in the means of communications: the men who made the new roads, bridges, canals, and railways were civilians, employed not by the

State, but by individuals, or companies of men, eager to develop the trade of the area from which they derived their personal incomes. Prominent among them were the large landed proprietors, and foremost of them Francis Egerton, the second Duke of Bridgewater, who, it is said, laid out more than a quarter of a million pounds on the development of his coal works and canals.

It was in 1759 that the Duke, tired of London society and disappointed in love, took up a project that his father had formed to construct a canal from his coal mines at Worsley to the growing town of Manchester, a few miles away. This was a work of considerable difficulty, since it involved, on the one hand, carrying the navigation into the underground workings, and, on the other, erecting an aqueduct over the Irwell at Barton. But the skill of James Brindley (1716–72), an unlettered millwright who had entered the Duke's service, overcame all obstacles; and by the summer of 1761 coal was being delivered to Manchester at a cost of carriage half that at which it had previously been brought by road. When the Seven Years War ended in 1763, and the rate of interest fell, the Duke embarked on the more ambitious enterprise of extending his canal to Runcorn at the mouth of the Mersey, and so of providing an efficient line of communication between the textile region of south-east Lancashire and Liverpool. Before the new waterway was opened in 1767, plans were already on foot for a canal which, passing through the salt-mining area of Cheshire and the pottery area of Staffordshire, would connect the Mersey with the Trent, and so with the Humber. This Grand Trunk, as it was called, was an undertaking the execution of which required far more capital than could be raised privately

The Duke, his brother-in-law, Earl Gower, Lord Anson, the Marquis of Stafford, Josiah Wedgwood, Richard Bentley, and others joined hands to secure the necessary Act and provide the resources. And Brindley again supplied the skill and organizing ability for an enterprise which brought under unified direction a larger body of men than had ever previously been employed in any single operation short of a military campaign. Many difficulties, physical and financial, were encountered: it was not until 1777, long after Brindley, worn out by his efforts, had gone to his grave, that the Grand Trunk was completed.

Meanwhile, the Wolverhampton Canal, begun in 1768, had linked the metal-working Midlands with the Severn: it had a junction with the Grand Trunk, and the two navigations together thus provided continuous transport by water between Bristol, Liverpool, and Hull. The next objective of the projectors was London. In 1767 and 1768 Acts had been obtained for two canals, the Coventry and the Oxford, which were to give access to the Thames. But the outbreak of the American War brought a sharp rise in the rate of interest that made it difficult to raise capital, and it was not until 1790 that this major aim was achieved. In the meantime several other canals had been cut in the region about Birmingham and in the North. But it was in the period of cheap capital of the early 'nineties that activity in construction reached its peak. The canal mania of 1790–4 undoubtedly led to some waste of national resources in ill-advised projects, but, taken as a whole, the investment in waterways brought, not only substantial dividends to shareholders, but an increase in the real income of the public in general.

The canal era was a short one—it coincided with the period 1760–1830—but it saw momentous changes in economic life. The cost of bulky or heavy commodities such as coal, iron, timber, stone, salt, and clay was greatly reduced; agricultural regions which had been remote from the market were brought within the widening circle of exchange; the fear of local famine, of both food and fuel, was removed; and the closer contact with others which the new means of communication afforded had a civilizing influence on the populations of the Potteries and other inland areas. There was a redistribution of activities: old river ports such as Bewdley and Bawtry declined, and new communities grew up at nodal points like Stourport. The competitive position of the more distant centres of production was improved, and rents in those nearer to the markets fell, or failed to rise as they must otherwise have done. The incomes paid out to those who dug the new canals, when spent, resulted in a raising of the level of employment generally. The offer of transferable shares, with prospects of high profit, accustomed men to invest their resources outside the restricted field of the Funds and the chartered trading companies, and so played a part in the rise of an impersonal market for capital. Perhaps the most important result, however, of the movement initiated by Bridgewater and Brindley was that it trained up a new race of engineers, equipped to meet the calls which the age of the railways was to make on their skill, endurance, and capacity for disciplined effort.

Parallel changes were made in the road system of Britain. In the first half of the century Acts had been passed to regulate such things as the weight of the load to be carried, the number of horses to a wagon, and the breadth of the rim of the wheels: the policy was one of making the traffic conform to the roads. After 1750, however, attempts were made to adapt the roads to the traffic. The number of turnpikes increased vastly, especially in the early 'fifties, and again in the early 'nineties, when rates of interest were low; and in the growing industrial regions of the North, in particular, several self-taught engineers did much to increase the carrying capacity of the highways. Among the pioneers was John Metcalf (1717–1810), who, in spite of blindness, constructed many new roads in Lancashire and York-shire, laying bunches of heather as a foundation where the sub-soil was soft, forming convex surfaces, and digging ditches to carry off the water which was the chief enemy of the road-maker, as of the miner. At a later stage came Thomas Telford (1757–1834), surveyor of the London-Holyhead road, architect of the beautiful Menai Bridge, and first President of the Society of Civil Engineers; and John Loudon Macadam (1756–1836), surveyor-general to the London turnpikes and the first great transport administrator. The methods of the two men were different: the first laid stress on solid founda-tions, the second on the use for the surface of broken stone or flint pressed so as to form a kind of arch. But, between them, they revolutionized travel. Wagons superseded pack-horses over much of the country; the number of public and private vehicles increased beyond measure; and, in the two decades that followed Waterloo, England passed into the era of flying coaches, busy way-side inns, and a preoccupation with the style and per-formance of horses that has not yet entirely disappeared. If the changes in the roads were of less moment to industry than those in the waterways, their effects on internal trade were significant; the commercial traveller came to take the place of the 'rider-out'; the Royal Mail became a more efficient channel of correspondence; and the processes of placing orders and remitting money were made more simple and speedy.

From early times it had been the practice at the larger collieries to lay down baulks of wood to facilitate the movement of the wagons that bore the coal to the river or the ports. In the early eighteenth century plates of cast iron were sometimes fixed to these at curves in the road or other points of exceptional friction. At a later stage, in 1767, Richard Reynolds constructed, from Coalbrookdale to the Severn, a track of cast-iron rails which were furnished with flanges to hold the wheels to the line; and in 1789, following the advice of the famous engineer, John Smeaton, the flange was transferred from the rail to the wheel. So far, the rails had been used almost exclusively about coal mines and iron works. But in 1801 the Surrey Iron Railway was constructed from Wandsworth to Croydon, to carry goods for the public in general. During the following twenty years about a score of companies were authorized to run tramways, most of which, however, acted as feeders to the canals rather than as alternative means of transport.

On all the early railroads traction was by horses. But from the 1760s many ingenious minds, in France as well as Britain, turned to the possibility of harnessing for carriage the newly discovered power of steam. In 1784 both William Symington and William Murdoch made model locomotives. But Watt, who was the arbiter on all matters relating to steam, looked on these as mere toys.

and, largely because of his obstructive attitude, the idea of steam locomotion was put aside. After the expiration of Watt's patent the Cornish engineer, Richard Trevithick (1771–1833), devised a high-pressure engine; and, in 1803, a steam carriage of his construction made several journeys through the streets of London. Public highways, however, proved to be unsuited to locomotive traffic, and Trevithick's bold experiment bore no immediate fruit. The possibility of running the engine on specially constructed roads was delayed by the curious belief that a smooth wheel would not 'bite' on a smooth rail: it was not until 1812 that a colliery engineer, William Hedley, demonstrated the practicability of a union of the two devices. Shortly afterwards, another colliery engine-wright, George Stephenson (1781–1848), raised the efficiency of the locomotive by increasing the draught to the fire-box; and when, in 1821, Edward Pease and his fellow Quakers obtained powers to construct a railway from Stockton to Darlington, Stephenson was engaged as engineer, and his locomotive (together with horses and cables wound by stationary engines) was used for traction. It was not, however, until 1829, when Stephenson's *Rocket* won the competition at Rainhill on the newly constructed Liverpool and Manchester Railway, that the potentialities of steam transport were fully realized. The locomotive railway was the culminating triumph of the technical revolution: its effects on the economic life of Britain and, indeed, of the world have been profound. But the unfolding of these—and of the parallel consequences of steam navigation—belongs to a period which falls beyond the limits of this book.

The production of engines was only one branch of that manufacture of machines which we call engineering.

The modern fitter, turner or pattern-maker can trace his pedigree back, beyond Stephenson, Watt, and Newcomen, to the millwright who was concerned with the creation and repair of water-wheels and the grinding apparatus which they worked. He can find ancestors, moreover, in the colliery viewers, clock-makers, instrument-makers, ironfounders and cotton spinners, who, during the industrial revolution, turned from using to making the appliances of their trades. An important step in the building up of a specialized industry was taken in 1795, when Boulton and Watt ceased to be mere consultants (supplying plans, supervising the construction of engines, and drawing royalties) and established the Soho Foundry at Birmingham. About the same time, or a little later, a number of engineering workshops were set up in London by men like Joseph Bramah, Henry Maudslay, and Joseph Clement. And in the textile centres of Lancashire and Yorkshire, where previously the master-spinners had made their own machines, there sprang up works like those of Dobson and Barlow, Asa Lees and Richard Roberts. Such establishments represented the external economies which are, at once, cause and effect of large-scale industry. The ingenious devices which flowed from them are too numerous to catalogue here: it must suffice to say that the more precise methods of planing, drilling, cutting, and turning which they developed played a significant part in the later phase of the technical revolution in Britain.

So far the process of invention has been traced first in one industry and then in another. The arrangement has the merit of making clear what was involved in each

uccessive step, but it fails to bring out the way in which
discoveries in different fields of activity were linked
together. Sometimes it was a simple case of imitation,
as when the principle of attenuating material by passing
it through rollers was transferred from the iron to the
textile industry, or when Wilkinson's method of boring
cannon was turned to the making of steam-engine
cylinders. Sometimes an advance in one sphere was a
condition of progress in another, as when the development of coke ovens made possible the extraction of tar.
Often two or more industries went hand in hand, each
contributing to the forward movement of the other.
Without the discovery of smelting with coke, which
made it possible to supply larger and more intricate
castings, Newcomen could not have perfected his
engine; and without Newcomen's engine Darby could
hardly have obtained the blast that was necessary to
produce iron on the scale required. Both the atmospheric and the steam engine helped to increase the output of coal and metals, and the larger supply of these
(and especially of copper and brass) reacted on the
development of engineering. 'Invention is the mother of
necessity': an improvement in one process frequently put
pressure on those concerned with an earlier, parallel, or
later process in the same industry. The invasion by the
founders of the territory of the forge-masters made these
look to new ways of reducing the cost of wrought iron;
the introduction of the fly shuttle made it imperative for
the spinners to seek out better methods of producing
yarn; and the later improvements in spinning and
weaving brought a new urgency to the search for
quicker methods of bleaching and finishing. In all these
ways innovation bred innovation.

G

The establishments at which each of the chief dis
coveries was first applied—Coalbrookdale, Cromford
Carron, Etruria, and Soho—became centres from which
ideas and enterprise radiated to other parts of the land
The Darbys gave a training to men like Joseph and
William Reynolds and the Cranage brothers; and from
the Carron Ironworks proceeded those of the Clyde
Calder, Crammond, and Muirkirk companies
Arkwright's technique, and his methods of organizing
labour, were copied by literally hundreds of master
cotton-spinners in England, Scotland, and Wales
Boulton and Watt gave instruction to a generation of
engineers which included Murdoch, Bull, Cameron
Southern, Ewart, and Brunton. And from a later school
of engineering, Henry Maudslay's works in London
came Nasmyth, Clement, Roberts, Whitworth, and
many more of their kind.

The development of invention is reflected in the table
of the Commissioners of Patents. Before the 1760s the
number of patents granted in any single year rarely ex
ceeded a dozen, but in 1766 it rose abruptly to 31, and in
1769 to 36. For some years the average remained
below this figure, but in 1783 there was a sudden jump to
64. Thereafter the number fell, until in 1792 another
bound brought it to 85. During the next eight years it
fluctuated about a mean of 67, but from 1798 an upward
movement brought it to a peak of 107 in 1802. Other
pinnacles appeared in 1813 and 1818, but these were no
outstanding. In 1824, however, the number of patent
shot up suddenly once more—to 180—and in the following
year of boom it attained the unprecedented height of
250. Those who take the perverse view that war is
spring of technological progress may be reminded that

each of the major peaks—1766, 1769, 1783, 1792, 1802, and 1824–5—came in a time of peace. And those who believe that the wind bloweth where it listeth may well ponder the fact that at each of these dates the rate of interest was below the prevailing level, and that at each of them expectations of profit were running high.

When the inventions are set in chronological order it is possible to detect one or two distinct phases. In the early years of the eighteenth century effort was directed mainly to the harnessing of forces external to man. At Coalbrookdale energy stored up in coal was the essential element in smelting, atmospheric pressure the power that worked the pumps, and gravitation the force by which the water, thus brought to a head, turned the great wheel which operated the bellows. From the thirties and 'forties, when capital was relatively abundant, and industrial workers still relatively scarce, attention was centred on labour-saving mechanisms, such as those of Kay and Paul in the textile industries; and the search continued until, in the 'sixties and 'seventies, it culminated in the appliances of Hargreaves, Arkwright, and Crompton. But by this time the nature of the economic problem was changing: population was beginning to press on resources. The quickening of the pace of enclosure and the breaking in of the waste were the outcome of a growing demand for food; Watt's first engine and the Duke's canals were the answer to a problem set by a shortage of coal; Cort's introduction of puddling and rolling was a measure to counter the continued famine of charcoal; and the researches of Dundonald and others may be thought of as the response of ingenuity to an insufficient supply of other raw materials. Towards the end of the century and later, when rates of interest were moving up, some (though by no means all) of the inventors turned their minds to capital-saving ends. The newer types of engine of Bull and Trevithick, and the newer ways of transmitting power, dispensed with much costly equipment; the newer methods of bleaching were economical of time; and the improved means of transport, with their greater speeds, released capital that had hitherto been locked up in goods on their way from producer to manufacturer, or manufacturer to consumer. It would be dangerous, however, to press these generalizations far. There was often a lag of years between an invention and its application, and it was this last, rather than the discovery itself, that was influenced by such things as a growing shortage of materials or a change in the supply of labour or capital. But, timing apart, it is important in each case to be clear whether the effect was to substitute natural resources or capital for labour, labour for capital, or one kind of labour for another. For on this depended the distribution, not merely among factors of production, but also among the different social classes of the increased wealth to which the inventions gave rise.

It should be borne in mind that the field in which innovation took place was only a part of the national economy: it covered little more than the industries concerned with appliances and those intermediate products, like yarn and cloth, that are included in the category of capital goods. The varied trades that provided things for the ultimate consumer were (apart from the pottery trade) hardly affected immediately. There were, in 1830, considerable areas of rural Britain, and many country towns, in which life went on in much the same

way as 100 years or more before. And even in the regions
about London, Manchester, and Birmingham there were
men and women who toiled laboriously, without the
aids that science and ingenuity had brought to their
fellows in the factory, the foundry, and the mine.

CHAPTER IV

CAPITAL AND LABOUR

I

THE industrial revolution was an affair of economics as well as of technology: it consisted of changes in the volume and distribution of resources, no less than in the methods by which these resources were directed to specific ends. The two movements were, indeed, closely connected. Without the inventions industry might have continued its slow-footed progress—firms becoming larger, trade more widespread, division of labour more minute, and transport and finance more specialized and efficient—but there would have been no industrial revolution. On the other hand, without the new resources the inventions could hardly have been made, and could never have been applied on any but a limited scale. It was the growth of savings, and of a readiness to put these at the disposal of industry, that made it possible for Britain to reap the harvest of her ingenuity.

There has been much discussion as to the origin of the capital that went into the expanding industries. Some say that it came from the land; others that it arose out of overseas trade; and yet others claim to have charted a current flowing from the secondary to the primary industries within the country. But for each piece of evidence it is possible to present counter-evidence. Many owners or occupiers of land, like Robert Peel, took to manufacture; but many successful manufacturers, like Arkwright, bought estates and finished as improving landlords. Many merchants, such as Anthony Bacon, reinvested their profits in mines or manufacture, but many industrialists, such as Sampson and Nehemiah Lloyd and Peter Stubs, began to market the things they produced and also to sell for others. Many craftsmen who worked in metal, like Abraham Darby, set up furnaces and forges and sank mines; but many miners and ironmasters pushed forward into the hardware and tool-making trades. If landowners like the Duke of Bridgewater put capital into turnpikes and canals, so also did manufacturers like Wedgwood. The currents flowed in all directions as wealth increased here, and opportunities there: it was from no single zone of thrift and enterprise that the trade winds blew.

In the early years of the period many of the industrial units were small family concerns or partnerships of two or three friends. In most industries the fixed capital required was not more than a domestic manufacturer, or even a workman, could supply from his earnings. If a profit were made it was possible to use it to extend the plant: 'ploughing back' is not, as some have supposed, a transatlantic discovery of the twentieth century. The early stages of accumulation can be illustrated by quotations from the diary of Samuel Walker of Rotherham:

1741. 'In or about October or November of the same year, Saml. and Aaron Walker built an Air Furnace in the old nailer's smithy, on the backside of Saml. Walker's cottage at Grenoside, making some small additions thereto, and another little hutt or two, slating with sods etc., with a small Garth walled in: and after rebuilding the chimney or stacks once, and the furnace once or more, began to proceed a little, Saml. Walker teaching the school at

Grenoside, and Aaron Walker making nails and mowing and shearing, etc., part of his time.'

1743. 'Aaron Walker now began to be pretty much imploy'd, and had 4 shillings a week to live upon. . . .'

1745. 'This year Saml. Walker, finding business increase, was obliged to give up his school, and built himself a house at the end of the old cottage, then thought he was fixed for life; then we allowed ourselves ten shillings a week each for wages to maintain our families.'

At this time the value of the concern was put at £400. But in the following year £100 was added by Jonathan Walker (a brother of Samuel and Aaron), £50 by John Crawshaw (who had previously been employed 'as much as we could, at 12 pence per day'), and £50 by Samuel himself. Thus equipped, the partners set up at Masborough first a casting house and then, in 1748, a steel furnace. The story that Samuel Walker rose to fortune by stealing from Huntsman the secret of crucible steel has no foundation: it was not by such methods, but by unremitting labour, thrift and integrity that success was achieved. Year after year some addition, great or small, was made to the plant. In 1754 a warehouse was built, and a keel—characteristically called *The Industry*—was put on the river. Four years later the partners dug 'a navigable cut' and 'improved the road from Holmes to Masbro' and lanes towards Tinsley—Gloria Deo'; and in 1764 they added to their establishment 'a large shop for frying pan makers'. It was not, apparently, until 1757, when the stock had reached £7,500, that the Walkers allowed themselves a dividend—of £140; and throughout, the proportion of the profit that was distributed remained small. Thus it came about that by

1774 the capital had reached £62,500. Profits on the manufacture of guns during the American War, ploughed back as they were, had, by 1782, raised the figure to £128,000. In this year Samuel Walker died, but the policy laid down by him was continued by his heirs, and in 1812 the assets of Samuel Walker & Co. were estimated at £299,015, and those of a sister concern, Walker and Booth, at a further £55,556.

Whatever may be said against the early employers, the charge of self-indulgence can hardly be laid at their door. The records of firm after firm tell the same story as that of the Walkers : the proprietors agreed to pay themselves small salaries, restrict their household expenses, and put their profits to reserves. It was in this way that Wedgwood, Gott, Crawshay, Newton Chambers & Co., and scores of others built up their great concerns. 'Industrial capital has been its own chief progenitor.'

From time to time, however, a business might require more funds than the most rigid economy could wring from internal sources. It was sometimes possible to obtain additional capital by taking in a new partner, active or sleeping. But the Bubble Act of 1720 restricted an ordinary partnership to six members, each of whom was liable 'to his last shilling and acre' for the debts of the concern, and it was not easy to induce men of substance to assume such risks. Hence it was more usual to raise resources by mortgaging the factory buildings to some neighbouring landowner, solicitor, clergyman, or widow. As the return on investment in the public Funds fell, a mortgage at 5 per cent. became an attractive security ; and throughout the industrial revolution— until, indeed, the coming of limited liability in the fifties and sixties of the nineteenth century—it remained an important instrument of industrial finance. Sometimes loans could be obtained, either in this way or on personal security, from friends or men engaged in the same field of activity: Abraham Darby provided capital for a number of fellow Quakers in the iron industry; Roebuck borrowed from Boulton, Arkwright from Strutt, and, later, Oldknow from Arkwright. But in the early years of the industrial revolution the market for long-term capital was generally local and confined.

Gradually, as the prospects of profits increased, the field of investment widened: men began to lend to enterprises further afield and to industries of which they knew little. In this process a large part was played by merchants, especially those of London, who, accustomed as they were to trust their goods to agents abroad, were often willing to embark part of their resources in industrial concerns at home. The early iron industry of South Wales, for example, was largely the creation of tea-dealers and other traders of London and Bristol, and the Clyde Valley owed much of its industrial equipment to the tobacco merchants of Glasgow. The transmutation of mercantile into fixed capital was an important cause (as well as a result) of the expansion of manufacture.

The industrialist needed not only long-term capital to set up and extend his works, but also working capital to cover the purchase of raw material, the cost of holding the product till it was paid for, and the sums to be handed over periodically to the wage-earners. The first of these short-term needs was generally met by the producer or the dealer—the wool-stapler, cotton merchant, ironmaster and so on—who provided the material on credit which ran into many months and often covered the full period of manufacture. The cost of maintaining stocks of finished goods, ready for delivery, and of bridging the gap between sale and payment was, however, burdensome. Here also long credits were the rule: throughout the eighteenth century it was usually six or twelve months, and sometimes even a couple of years or more, before a manufacturer was paid for his wares. With the speeding-up of transport and communications there was a tendency to shorten the accommodation; and the rise in rates of interest that followed the outbreak of the war with France in 1793 strengthened the practice of giving discounts for prompt payment and charging interest on overdue accounts. A new sense of time was one of the outstanding psychological features of the industrial revolution.

The payment of wages at more or less regular intervals meant that the employer had not only to find funds, but find them in a form acceptable to the wage-earner. Gold guineas, or even half-guineas, were of a value too high to be of much use for the purpose; and, since the currency reforms of 1697 and 1717 had left silver undervalued in terms of gold, there was a tendency for it to leave the circulation. During the course of the century very little silver came into Britain: only small quantities were minted, and large amounts of coin were melted down and sent abroad, by the East India Company in particular. The dearth of coin of small denomination was a serious matter for manufacturers with wages to pay. Many of them spent days riding from place to place in search of shillings. Some effected economies by taking over from the earlier form of industry the practice of the 'long-pay'. And at least one cotton-spinner of the early nineteenth century met the situation by staggering the payment of wages. Early in the morning a third of the employees were paid and sent off to make their household purchases; within an hour or two the money had passed through the hands of the shop-keepers and was back at the factory ready for a second group of workers to be paid and sent off; and in this way before the day was over all had received their wages and done their buying in. Other manufacturers, less ingenious, or less well-situated, resorted to payment in truck: a practice especially common with those remote from the towns. Others, again, like John Wilkinson and the Anglesey Copper Company, minted their own token coins and paid these to their workers. When, during the Napoleonic War, inflation led to a veritable famine of small change, employers, like Robert Peel and Samuel Oldknow, took to paying wages in bills or small notes which the local shopkeepers were willing to accept on the guarantee of the issuer that he would meet them with a bill on London at a later date. All these practices were objectionable. The abuses to which the truck system was open are obvious: the tokens and shop-notes were often taken by the retailer only at a discount; and wherever wages were paid other than in coin of the realm the employer was in effect shifting his function of providing working capital on to the wage-earners, the shopkeepers, or, where the notes or tokens passed into circulation, the community at large. In many cases, however, he had little or no choice in the matter. The fault lay not, as is sometimes supposed, in cupidity or ill-will on his part, but in defects of the monetary system for which the Government itself was responsible.

If there had been a properly constituted system of banking much of the difficulty might have been avoided. There was, it is true, the Bank of England, which had been set up as early as 1694. But this tended to concentrate its activities on providing accommodation for the State and the merchants and trading companies of the Metropolis. Although, in 1708, it had been given a monopoly of joint-stock note issue for England and Wales, it was unwilling to open branches, and hence few of the notes reached the industrial areas. (It was, as has been said, the Bank of London, rather than of England.) There were also in the capital old-established businesses, like those of the Childs and Hoares, which had become merchant banks; but these were concerned mainly with dealings in bullion and foreign exchange, raising loans for governments at home and abroad, and accepting, or guaranteeing, bills of exchange drawn by traders who had opened accounts with them. They too (until 1770) issued notes, but these, like those of the Bank, were of high denomination and unsuited to the needs of the manufacturers.

For the larger transactions of commerce the instrument was the bill of exchange, drawn by a creditor on a debtor who accepted it for payment three, six, or twelve months ahead. Bills could be passed from hand to hand, and, endorsed by each holder in turn, gained repute in proportion to the number of transactions in which they played a part: in Lancashire bills, often for quite small sums, formed by far the greater part of the medium of circulation. For payments at a distance, however, it was often necessary that the bill should bear a name with a reputation in London and so in the country at large. In the first half of the eighteenth century, and indeed earlier, a country merchant was often willing, on payment of a commission, to supply bills, drawn on his London house or correspondent, to other traders who had payments to make in the Metropolis or elsewhere.

And similarly he was willing to buy, at a discount, bills which traders or manufacturers had drawn on their customers, and in this way to provide guineas and smaller coin to those who needed them for the payment of wages or other purposes. Sometimes he put up on his door a notice that he was willing to extend these and other facilities to accredited clients, and so he became a banker.

As far as is known, the first provincial banking house was that set up, in 1716, by James Wood, a soap and tallow dealer of Bristol, but it was not until after 1760 that private banks of this kind became general. They had no common origin. Vaughan of Gloucester began as a goldsmith, Gurney of Norwich as a worsted manufacturer, and Smith of Nottingham as a mercer. In the agricultural districts of England the local corn merchant often graduated into banking; and in Wales a number of drovers set up at Llandovery an institution known as the Bank of the Black Ox, and at Aberystwyth another called the Bank of the Black Sheep (a title which, it should be added, cast no aspersion on the proprietors, but arose from the fact that their £1 note bore on it a picture of a black sheep, and their 10s. note one of a black lamb). As manufacture increased, many industrialists—the Arkwrights, Wilkinsons, Walkers, and the firm of Boulton and Watt among them—established banks of their own, partly, no doubt, as a means of obtaining cash for wages and bills for remittances, but partly as an outlet for their growing capital. It was from manufacturing sources that Lloyds, Barclays, and other well-known concerns came into being.

By 1793 the country banks numbered about 400, and by 1815 (including some branches) about 900. Each was a relatively small concern, for the law prevented the rise of joint-stock companies; and, even if an Act of incorporation could have been obtained, the privilege granted to the Bank of England made it impossible for any other corporate body to issue notes. Each, however, had a London correspondent bank on which it, or its customers, could draw, and from which notes and coin could be obtained by discounting bills. Some transferred their business to the Metropolis or set up separate banking concerns there, and in this way there arose such well-known London houses as Smith, Payne and Smith, Jones, Lloyd & Co., and Taylor, Lloyd and Bowman. In 1760 there had been between twenty and thirty banks in London: by 1800 there were seventy. It was by bankers' drafts on these (bills drawn by one banker on another) that large-scale business was conducted.

When an ordinary bank made a loan to a client it either provided him with a bill or draft, or paid out to him coin, or, more frequently, its own promissory notes. In rural areas and in most centres of industry other than Lancashire, the notes of the banker became the chief form of money. Against his issue of notes the banker had to keep a reserve of coin, but this was generally small, for if he needed more he could obtain it by sending bills to his agent in London, and the agent, in turn, could replenish his store by sending bills to the Bank of England. All went well so long as the Bank of England was willing to lend freely. But there were occasions when, owing to the overriding demands of the Government or other circumstances, it was obliged to restrict its discounts, and when, therefore, large numbers of local banks were unable to pay out cash, and had to close their doors. The lives of most private banks were short. The fortunes of all were bound up with those of a particular area. Some bankers used the money of depositors for their own trading or speculative purposes. Some were slow to learn what has been called the first lesson of banking—how to distinguish between a bill and a mortgage—and when, as often happened, there was a sudden demand for cash they found themselves with assets locked up in long-terms loans. In 1772, 1793, 1814–16, and 1825, in particular, large numbers of them went down, carrying with them to the Bankruptcy Court many manufacturers and traders, and causing loss to all who held their notes.

As time went on it became clear that the small private banks with their limited resources were unable to meet the needs of a factory economy. They were accused of responsibility for the inflation of 1793–1815, and when, in the years of slump that followed the war, large numbers of them failed, they were regarded not merely as the victims, but also as the authors, of the disasters. In the early 'twenties Thomas Joplin and others pointed out that Scotland, where joint-stock banks were allowed, had been free from financial adversity. And when, in 1826, an inquest was held on the crisis of the preceding year, Parliament decided to permit the setting up of corporate banks in England outside a radius of sixty-five miles of London. The same enthusiasm and local patriotism as had gone to the making of the canals and early railways were brought to the formation of new institutions such as the Manchester and Liverpool District Banking Company, which drew their capital and deposits from a wide field, had many branches, and were able to spread their loans over a variety of industries. At the same time the Bank of England reluctantly yielded

o the pressure of Lord Liverpool and began to open
note-issuing branches in the provinces. The manufac-
urers of the 'thirties and 'forties had their difficulties
o contend with, but a persistent shortage of liquid
esources was no longer one of these.

When the Duke of Bridgewater was constructing his
canal he drew £25,000 from Child & Co.; when
Arkwright was setting up his frames he obtained sub-
tantial help from Wright of Nottingham; when, in 1778,
Matthew Boulton was heavily involved in engine-
building in Cornwall, he had a credit of £14,000 from
Lowe, Vere & Co. of London, and shortly afterwards
borrowed £2,000 from Elliot and Praed of Truro.
In spite of these and many other instances that might
be cited, it is doubtful whether the banking system
was a principal source of the capital by which the
new technique was applied to manufacture. It seems
likely that bankers played a larger part in the extension
than in the initiation of firms, and that the securities
they held were mortgages and bonds, rather than shares
involving participation in the risks of industry. Common
sense alone would have dictated a cautious policy, for the
mortality of businesses was high. But the law of partnership was also a determining factor. Large enterprises
concerned with public works—turnpikes, canals, docks,
bridges, and waterworks—were able to obtain the
privilege of incorporation: a banker was often willing to
take shares in these, since he had the knowledge that he
could dispose of his holding to others if need arose. But
Parliament was generally unwilling to concede the same
right to manufacturing firms; and, short of becoming a
partner, with all that this implied in trouble and risk,
there was no way in which the banker could participate

H

in them. He was a creditor rather than a partner of th manufacturer.

The chief contribution of the banks to the industria revolution consisted in the mobilizing of short-term func and their transfer from areas where there was little de mand for them to others that were hungry for capital. I the agricultural counties landlords, farmers, and dealer paid in to the local banks the bills and cash they receive as rent or payment for produce (they were paid intere on the sum deposited or were given interest-bearin notes). The banks remitted the bills to their corre pondent bank in London which, after collecting then found itself with considerable funds. These it used t discount bills for banks in industrial centres, which wer thus in turn able to lend to their clients currency, in th form of drafts or bills on London, or cash. The move ment took place mainly in the late autumn and earl winter, when the crops were being sold; but this was th very time when the manufacturers, who settled thei accounts at the end of the year, were most in need funds. The marriage between the thrift of the South an East and the enterprise of the Midlands and the Nort was both happy and fertile. It meant in effect that rura England was providing foodstuffs for the growing urba communities without requiring an immediate returi and that industrial England was thus able to use its ow resources to put up factories and construct canals an railways which benefited manufacturing and agricu tural areas alike.

Many institutions besides the banks helped in th process of mustering and distributing capital. In 177 the Stock Exchange, which had previously consisted of group of brokers meeting in a coffee-house, obtaine premises of its own: its first List, issued in 1803, showed that its dealings were no longer confined to the Funds and East India stock, but covered also that of public utility and insurance companies. In London there arose specialist bill-brokers, like Richardson, Overend & Co., and finance houses such as those of the Goldsmids, Ricardos, Barings, and Rothschilds; and in the provinces country solicitors increasingly acted as intermediaries for mortgages, annuities, and stock. Insurance (marine, fire, and life) was a powerful instrument for assembling the savings of the middle classes; and those of the workers went largely into friendly societies, the number of which, by 1800, ran into several thousands. From 1798, if not before this, philanthropists, anxious to inculcate a spirit of independence and reduce resort to the parish, had set up savings banks for the working classes: by 1819 there were over 350 of these in various parts of the kingdom, and by 1828 their combined deposits amounted to more than 14 million pounds.

In 1760 Britain was already investing resources abroad, in 'factories' in India, and plantations in the West Indies. But on balance, it seems likely, she was a net importer of capital. Though the long-term rate of interest here had fallen, it was still well above that of Holland, and Dutch bankers and merchants found it profitable to take up investments in England rather than in their own country. Some of them lent direct to English industrialists—in 1769 Matthew Boulton borrowed £8,000 in Amsterdam—but more often they put their money into government, Bank of England, or East India funds. In the middle years of the eighteenth century it was believed that foreigners, mainly Dutch, held about a third of these stocks; and in 1776, according to an

estimate attributed to Lord North, about three-seventh
of the British National Debt was in their hands. Thi
meant that an equivalent amount of native resources wa
freed for investment elsewhere. Foreign capital played a
not unimportant role in the early stages of the industria
revolution.

In the course of the American War, however, Hollanc
became involved in hostilities with Britain, and Dutcl
capital was repatriated. Amsterdam never recovered the
loss she suffered at this time, and before the end of the
century London had taken her place as the leading
centre for international loans. During the wars of 1793–
1815 British capital flowed to Europe, as loans or sub-
sidies to allies : there was much investment in the United
States and, from 1806, in South America. After 181
British investors, operating through Barings, Rothschilds
and others, were active in French *rentes* and, as one writer
has said, 'all the principal European states found i
possible to drown their sorrows by imbibing freely the
draught of British capital'. In the early 'twenties, when
rates of interest in this country were low, there was a
large efflux of funds to the newly enfranchised colonies
of Spain, as well as to Greece. Over the period 1816–2
(according to an estimate made in 1827) Britain lent
some 93 million pounds to foreign nations, in addition to
smaller amounts invested in mining and trading concerns and carried abroad in the pockets of emigrants.

In 1760 there was nothing that could justly be called a
capital market. Lending was still largely a local and
personal matter. By 1830 the volume of investable funds
had grown beyond measure. Banks, and other institutions, served as pools from which capital, brought by in-
numerable streams, flowed to industries at home and

broad. Instead of the guess, shrewd or ill-founded, as to the credit-worthiness of the borrower, there was, for part of the field, the published List as a guide. Capital was becoming impersonal—'blind', as some say—and highly mobile.

II

The considerations that led employers to draw people into a single place of work were diverse. In the iron industry the mechanics of smelting and rolling were such that it was virtually impossible to produce on a small scale, and in the cotton industry there was obvious advantage in providing power for a large number of operatives from a single water-wheel or engine. In other cases the reasons were economic rather than technological. On grounds of quality it was essential that the manufacture of chemicals and machinery should be subject to oversight: it was the need for supervision of work that led Peter Stubs to gather the scattered file-makers into his works at Warrington. In the pottery trade the economies to be derived from division and sub-division of labour were the chief inducement to the creation of Wedgwood's Etruria. And in the woollen industry the necessity of putting a stop to embezzlement of material was the main incentive to aggregation in the mills of Benjamin Gott. What is fairly clear is that there was no strong desire on the part of the workers themselves to congregate in large establishments. It was only under the impact of powerful forces, attractive and repellent, that the English labourer or craftsman was transformed into a factory hand.

In the eighteenth century there were many impediments to the movement of labour, whether from place to place or from one occupation to another. Difficulties of transport played only a minor part, for, though the highways might be unsuited to heavy traffic, they were generally good enough for people who travelled on foot. It was not always safe, however, for a man to take to the road, since there were times when he was liable to be picked up by a press-gang, or kidnapped and sent to the Plantations. When James Watt was learning his trade in London in 1756, he was afraid to go abroad in the streets, and when, nearly a quarter of a century later, William Murdoch was sent from Birmingham to Cornwall, it was necessary to provide him with special protection.

More serious were the obstacles that arose from the operation of the Poor Law, and especially from the conditions of settlement. If a man left the parish in which he was domiciled, and remained in another for a full year, he lost his right to relief in the first and established a claim to it in the second. For this reason parish authorities were reluctant to receive outsiders, and employers who were large ratepayers would sometimes offer work only for a period short of a full year. If before a labourer had gained a settlement in a new parish he fell on evil days he could be moved back summarily to the parish from which he had come, and this made him think twice before leaving his native village to seek work far away. After 1795 many parishes in the South, following the policy of the magistrates of Speenhamland, began to give outdoor relief according to a scale based on the price of bread and the size of the family. There was nothing to object to in this: it was only sensible and humane to see that the income of the poor did not fall below the minimum of subsistence. But many of the authorities, confusing the problem of the wage-earner

with that of the pauper, undertook to make up from the
rates the amount by which the wages of the labourer fell
short of their standard. A grant of relief that varies in-
versely with earnings is the worst form of subsidy, since
it destroys the incentive for the worker to demand, or the
employer to offer, higher wages. It led to an over-
population of the agricultural villages, similar to that
which existed on a larger scale in Ireland, and (what is
to the present purpose) reduced the pressure on the
labourers to move.

Industrial practices inherited from early times were
also a deterrent. In corporate towns it was illegal to
engage in a skilled occupation without first having served
as an apprentice; and, even outside these, most children
who wanted to have a trade at their finger ends—and
many who had no such aspiration—were bound for six
or seven years, and made liable to penalties if they left
their employer before the end of the period. Nor was it
only the young who were tied in this way. In the coal
industry of Scotland all classes of workers were literally
serfs, bound by law and custom to a laird, and subject to
purchase and sale with the pits; and in Northumberland
and Durham, and some other English coalfields, the men
were still engaged at annual hirings under bonds which
ran just short of the year. One of the biggest problems
that confronted the employers of the early years of the
industrial revolution was that of selecting men capable
of learning the new techniques and susceptible to the
discipline that the new forms of industry imposed. When
time and energy had been given to this it was only
prudent to ensure that the trainee would not be enticed
away. Boulton and Watt made their engine-erectors
enter into agreements to serve for three or five years; the

Earl of Dundonald contracted with one of his chemical workers for twenty-five years; and some of the iron-founders in South Wales were tied for the term of their natural lives.

When an employer sought to engage a man from another district he often failed because he was unable to offer work to other members of the family. To surmount this difficulty ironmasters, like those at Backbarrow, sometimes set up textile works near their furnaces so as to provide employment for the women and children. Conversely, when an employer, like Oldknow or Greg, wanted juvenile or female labour, he was sometimes obliged to extend his operations to agriculture, lime-burning and so on, in order to find work for the men. The industrial unit was often not a single establishment but something approaching a colonial settlement.

The problem can best be illustrated by a survey of employment in the cotton industry. When Arkwright's water-frame thrust its way into a trade organized on a household basis there was much hasty improvisation. Early attempts to obtain adult labour proved futile. It had been the practice of many Poor Law authorities to assemble paupers in houses of industry and set them to spinning and other simple tasks; hence it was not un-natural that the new factories should be thought of as workhouses and given a wide berth by the independent labourer. The geographical situation of the mills was such that, in any case, only a small fraction of the labour could be drawn from local sources. It was unthinkable that the male weaver would leave his loom and take to work of less skill as a spinner, and it was equally unthink-able that his wife and children would leave their home for the country factory. But there was, especially in London and the South, a large supply of unskilled, unemployed people who were a charge on the parishes, and in many places the growing burden of the rates led the overseers to offer to transfer batches of children, or whole families, to factories in the North. It was by such means that the cotton masters obtained a large part of their labour.

The story of the factory 'apprentices' is a depressing one. The children, many of them only seven years of age, had to work twelve, or even fifteen, hours a day, for six days a week. As Mr. and Mrs. Hammond have said, 'their young lives were spent, at best in monotonous toil, at worst in a hell of human cruelty'. Employers who took their responsibilities seriously—the Arkwrights, the Gregs, Samuel Oldknow and, above all, Robert Owen—provided not only board in pleasant and well-designed 'prentice houses (such as can still be seen at Styal and Mellor) but also the rudiments of an education. The children were able to play in the fields, and some had little gardens of their own. Care was taken to keep the sexes apart (a visitor to the Cressbrook factory in Millers Dale was told that instruction in singing was given to the boys, but not to the girls, though 'as the girls' rooms were immediately above the boys', the sweet sounds would ascend and the girls participate in the harmony'). Several of the boys at the Gregs' factory at Styal rose to managerial posts, and at least half a dozen of Oldknow's apprentices afterwards set up as spinners on their own account. But at many other places, as at Backbarrow, the tale is one of neglect, promiscuity, and degradation.

When, in 1816, the first Sir Robert Peel was asked about apprentice labour he said: '. . . At the time when

Arkwright's machinery had first an existence, steam power was but little known, and . . . those who wished to carry on their business, and benefit by these improvements, resorted to country places where there were great waterfalls, and consequently could not have any other than apprentice labour; and I was in that situation, for I had no other.' A modern might have retorted that he had the alternative of refusing to adopt the new technique at all. But the modern would be passing judgement according to the code of an age which (because of the industrial revolution) has a standard of life immeasurably higher than that of Peel's day, and which (partly because children are now in short supply) sets a different value on child life. The conduct of the factory masters must be judged in the light of their own age and of that which preceded it. It was not very long since Jonas Hanway had remarked that 'few parish children live to be apprenticed'. Those who did live had been put out to tradesmen and others, and many had suffered miseries certainly no less than those of the factory children. It must be remembered, also, that the employers were, like their forbears, essentially merchants. David Dale (we have it on the authority of Robert Owen) did not visit his factory more than once in two or three months; and the vagueness of the answers that other cotton masters gave to questions put to them by committees of inquiry arose less, perhaps, from a consciousness that there was something to hide, than from sheer ignorance of conditions in their own works. The superintendents they appointed to their factories were largely technicians concerned with the running of the plant, and the administration of labour was lax. Not until the industrial revolution was well on

ts way did there arise a body of men capable of perform-
ing some at least of the functions of the labour manager
of to-day.

In spite of a widespread impression to the contrary, the
period 1760–1830 saw an increased concern for human
unhappiness, and especially for that of the young—even
on the part of the cotton men. It was Peel who, stimulated by a Manchester physician, Thomas Percival,
pressed on Parliament the need for regulation of the
factories. His Act of 1802—the Health and Morals of
Apprentices Act—limited hours of work and prescribed
minimum standards of hygiene and education. It is true
that it was passed only when the worst was over, and that
neither it nor Peel's second Act of 1819 (which applied
to all children, pauper or 'free') went very far. But at
least the basis was laid for that code of legislation which
is one of the corner-stones of modern industrial society.

Not all who worked in the country factories were
parish apprentices. At Arkwright's three mills in
Derbyshire, in 1789, about two-thirds of the 1,150
workers were children, but at other establishments, a
few years later, the proportion was somewhat lower. For
the adults it was necessary to put up houses, shops, and
places of worship, and so there arose small communities
in which, as time went on, men and women were able,
in some measure, to direct their own lives. As the
children grew up and had families of their own the
practice of drawing on the overseers declined, and the
factories came to be staffed by free labour.

The women and children who had spun on the jenny
in their own homes found it difficult to compete with the
power-driven machines, and, from the early 'nineties,
many began to learn from their menfolk how to weave

the calicoes, muslins, and cambrics that were now demanded. At the same time the steam engine and the mule were being applied to the spinning of cotton. The first made it possible to set up factories in the towns, where labour was more plentiful, and the second created a need for a new type of labour in spinning. The mule called for both strength and skill beyond that of a child, and many of the weavers now handed over their loom to their wives and took to factory employment. The occupations of the sexes were reversed, but the family economy remained intact.

As places of work the town factories were no more eligible than those of the country. There was the same dearth of managers and overlookers, and many of the women and children were hired and directed by the male spinners. But the proportion of the very young employed in them was lower than that in the water driven mills of the older pattern. In 1816 at the country factory of Samuel Greg, of a total of 252 workers, 17 per cent. were under ten, and not quite 30 per cent. above eighteen, years of age. A few miles away in Manchester M'Connel and Kennedy were giving employment to 1,020 people, of whom only 3 per cent. were under ten, and 52 per cent. were above eighteen. Even in the town factory, however, it is clear that a large part of the labour consisted of young people. The reliance on workers of tender years was partly the result of technological change and partly of the fact that (as Dr. Ure put it) it was 'nearly impossible to convert persons past the age of puberty, whether drawn from rural or from handicraft occupations, into useful factory hands'.

In the early decades of the nineteenth century weaving began to follow spinning and became a factory process.

But whereas the water-twist and mule-spinning factories had sprung up almost overnight, the power-operated weaving mills came very slowly. This was due partly to imperfections in the power-loom itself, partly to the long war with France (which, by raising the rate of interest, discouraged investment in plant), and partly to the reluctance of the weavers, many of them women, to leave their homes. With peace and the falling rates of interest of the 'twenties, many master spinners came to attach weaving sheds to their mills; but it was not until after 1834, when the austerity of the new Poor Law was brought to bear on the semi-starved weavers, that the full triumph of the factory was assured. As the power-looms increased in number the demand for domestic weavers declined; but the supply of these was maintained by an influx of Irish who, content with low standards of living, were even less patient than the English of the discipline of the factory. It is sometimes suggested that the 'evils' of the industrial revolution were due to the rapidity with which it proceeded: the case of the domestic textile workers suggests the exact opposite. If there had been in weaving a man of the type of Arkwright, if rates of interest had remained low, if there had been no immigration and no Poor Law allowance, the transfer to the factory might have been effected quickly and with less suffering. As it was, large numbers of hand workers continued, for more than a generation, to fight a losing battle against the power of steam. In 1814 the price paid for weaving a piece of calico by hand had been 6s. 6d.; by 1829 it had fallen to 1s. 2d.

The plight of overworked apprentices and under-employed domestic weavers does not constitute the full story of the revolution in textiles. It is not necessary to

accept as evidence the picture drawn by the egregiou
Dr. Ure of the 'lively elves' whose work in the factory
'seemed to resemble a sport', in order to believe that, al
in all, the effect of the inventions was to lighten labour
Most of the factory operatives were engaged at rates o
pay which raised family incomes above those of any
earlier generation. As women and girls became less de
pendent on their menfolk they gained in self-respect and
in public esteem. As the factories moved to the towns, or
towns grew up about the factories, the practice of the
long pay gave way to weekly or fortnightly disburse
ments, and truck and the indebtedness of workers to
employers declined. Since the operatives were no longer
isolated cottagers it was easier for them to form union
to defend their standards of hours and wages; and it
became possible to enlist in the fight against abuses, the
force of a public opinion which, through the medium o
church and chapel and the Press, was becoming increasingly vocal.

In other industries the course of change, though less
spectacular, was similar to that in textiles. In coal
mining, as in cotton-spinning, the central problem was
that of obtaining an adequate supply of labour, and
many of the devices that were introduced were aimed at
enabling boys and youths to do work that had previously
been done by experienced pitmen. Some enlightened
Scottish owners, including Dundonald and Sir John
Sinclair, had liberated their collier-serfs; and, by Acts o
Parliament passed in 1774 and 1799, the lifetime
bondage of Scottish miners in general was brought to an
end. The motive was, no doubt, mainly humanitarian
but some of the employers had supported emancipation

by urging that it would raise the status of the coal-getter and so draw into the industry new supplies of labour. Their hopes proved vain. Many of the liberated colliers moved out, some to the ironworks, some to the army, and some to England—though not to the mines of Northumberland and Durham, which were too deep and dangerous to attract the Scots, even if the pitmen had been willing to allow them to come in.

In this northern English coalfield the miners formed a compact, self-contained community. They were pro-lific, and, since sons almost invariably followed their fathers to the pits, the number of workers increased steadily. But, as the industrial revolution proceeded, and as, with the improvements in transport, markets widened, the demand for coal grew more rapidly than the supply of colliers. The effect was registered in a rise of wages and, even more, in an increase of the premium paid to the pitmen at the annual hirings. During the first half of the eighteenth century this had amounted to only a few shillings, but in 1764 it rose to three or four guineas, and in 1804 (a year of boom) to as much as eighteen guineas, a head. It is to the credit of the pitman that he used his increased income to withdraw his womenfolk from the mines. (There is no recorded in-stance of women or girls working underground in the northern field after 1780.) But the rise in the wages of the adult miner gave an impetus to the use of boys, who were employed, in increasing numbers, to open and shut the doors that regulated the currents of air, to drag the corves from the face to the main passages, and to drive the ponies along these to the pit bottom.

In the smaller coalfields of England and Wales, where development was slower and pits smaller, less use (so it seems) was made of child labour, but, on the other hand, women continued to work below ground. It is sometimes suggested that the presence of women in an industry has a humanizing effect on the men who work in it; but one would need to take a very optimistic view of the nature of man to believe that this was true of coal mining. The evils brought to light in the reports of the early 'forties have sometimes been laid at the door of the industrial revolution, but, like so many other abuses, they went back to a more primitive stage of production and were, in fact, tending to disappear.

The improvements in spinning, weaving, and mining were broadly of a labour-saving character: they enabled a few workers to achieve results that had previously required many, and children to perform tasks that had formerly been set to men or women. But output was so much enlarged that, in spite of this, the earnings of most of the adults were increased. There were other industries in which progress followed a different course. In engineering (civil and mechanical) and in the manufacture of iron, chemicals, and pottery the problem was that, not of finding semi-skilled labour to tend machines, but of training up men in the new techniques. Much of the time of the inventors themselves was taken up in this way. Brindley had been obliged to begin his task with the aid of miners and common labourers, but in the process of constructing his canals he created new classes of tunnellers and navvies of high skill. In his early days Watt had to make shift with the millwrights—men who could turn from one job to another and were willing to work alike in wood, metal, or stone, but were hide-bound by tradition: before he died there had come into being

pecialized fitters, turners, pattern-makers, and other
grades of engineers. The first generation of cotton-
spinners had themselves employed 'clock-makers' to construct and repair their frames and mules; but gradually
these were replaced by highly trained textile machinists
and maintenance men. Cort's innovations meant that
the craftsmanship of the finers and hammermen was no
longer required, but they demanded a dexterity no less
great from the puddlers and rollermen whom he himself
trained. If Wedgwood split up the manufacture of
pottery into a score of separate processes, each of these
required its own special aptitude, and some a high
degree of artistic talent. Nor was this access of skill at
the expense of the handicrafts that remained outside the
field of large-scale industry. The building of the factories
called for proficiency from bricklayers, masons, and
carpenters, and their equipment for the craftsmanship of
spindle-makers, filesmiths, and a host of others who
worked individually or in small concerns. The state-
ment, sometimes made, that the industrial revolution
was destructive of skill is not only untrue, but the exact
reverse of the truth.

In this group of industries the organization of production was at first even more loose than that of the cotton
mills. The canals and railways were built by a chain of
contractors and sub-contractors who employed gangs of
navvies and labourers with little control by the engineer
who was responsible for the enterprise as a whole. In
the metal trades the journeyman system of sub-letting
continued long after the workers had been brought to a
common place of employment. In the iron industry the
melters and founders engaged their own apprentices
and paid their own labourers. And in the manufacture

I

of pottery (where the typical undertaking was not
factory but a number of workshops grouped together
the boy pressers, turners, and platemakers were inden
tured to, or hired by, the workmen themselves. Whethe
the young or unskilled were well or badly treate
depended very much on the character of the gang
master or artisan for whom they worked. But since, i
most of these occupations, innovation was largely of
capital-saving nature, its effect was to increase not onl
output but also the share of the value of this that wen
to the worker. In income, at least, the gain to labou
can hardly be in doubt.

As the capital embodied in building and appliance
increased, it became a matter of concern to the owner
that it should not stand idle unnecessarily. In mos
occupations hours of work were from dawn to dusk
with short halts for breakfast and dinner. Punctuality i
beginning or resuming work was a prime industria
virtue, and the clock, which had a prominent place o
the face of the factory, was at once an aid to rectitud
and a witness to default. (There is a well-attested stor
that when the Duke of Bridgewater reproved his me
for being late in returning after the midday break the
excused themselves by saying that they had failed t
hear the stroke of one: the Duke immediately had th
clock altered so that henceforth it struck thirteen.) A
Etruria, from Lady Day to Michaelmas, the bell rang a
5.45 and work began at six; for the rest of the year i
sounded a quarter of an hour before daybreak, and worl
continued until it was no longer possible to see. But i
1792 William Murdoch demonstrated the possibility o
using coal gas as an illuminant, and from the early year
of the new century many factories and works were ru

rough the hours of dark. Whether the working time
as longer or shorter than that of the domestic craftsman
impossible to say: it can hardly have been longer than
at of the nail-workers who (according to Thomas
ttwood in 1812) worked from four in the morning till
n at night.

The second generation of employers—such as the
ounger Boulton, Watt, Wedgwood, or Crawshay—was
erhaps more alive than the first to the losses that might
rise from irregularity or carelessness on the part of
bour. Men trained in the concern were appointed as
anagers and foremen; piece-rates and bonus schemes
ere introduced to stimulate effort; and fines were
nposed for drunkenness, sloth and gaming. The new
ethods of administration, the new incentives, and the
ew discipline' were as much a part of the revolution as
e technical inventions themselves: adaptation to them
as the price the workers had to pay for the higher
comes that large-scale industry brought.

The hand-loom weavers, stockingers, nail-makers, and
e labourers of the agricultural South, were slow to
espond to economic change. And there were others who
-whether from inertia, conservatism, or an understand-
ble wish to control their own lives—refused to conform
the new order. They, too, paid their price. But as the
gours of the laws of settlement were relaxed, and as news
f the earnings to be made in the factories was spread
by the Press, the town crier, and most often, by ordinary
ord of mouth) the drift to the rising centres of manu-
acture increased. The movement of individuals was
enerally over only a short distance: from the Cheshire
ountryside to the Lancashire town, from the outlying

parts of Staffordshire or Worcestershire to Birmingham from the Peak district to Sheffield, or from one valley South Wales to the next. In the areas from which th migrants had gone a shortage of labour caused wages rise, and hence people from farther afield moved in these. As Professor Redford has shown, a series of shor waves of migration achieved in the end the effect of long wave, rolling from the South and East to th Midlands and the North.

There was, however, one long-distance movement tha was direct. The attractive power of English wages, an the repellent force of hunger—especially in the famine of 1782–4 and 1821–3—brought large numbers of Iris men and women, from their sub-divided holdings, t seek work or subsistence in Britain. Arrived here, som simply swelled the body of paupers; but some took t harvesting, hop-picking, and other forms of agricultura work—and, after having saved a few pounds, declare themselves penniless and got the Poor Law authorities t give them a free passage home. Many, however, re mained in Britain. Some were employed in the heavy an less skilled occupations of building and coal-heaving but the majority made a living by work in textiles, eithe as spinners at Glasgow and Paisley, or as hand-loo weavers in England. Their Celtic impetuosity, impati ence of authority, and gifts of speech, were not withou effect on industrial relations (and, in particular, on th character and methods of trade unions) in the later year of the industrial revolution in Lancashire.

The influx of the Irish was offset (and perhaps mor than offset) by an exodus of English and Scots overseas The movement of artisans had been prohibited by series of statutes aimed at preventing knowledge

British processes from reaching possible competitors in
Europe and America; and employers, including Samuel
Garbett and Josiah Wedgwood, had been active in
prosecuting would-be emigrants and those who tried to
seduce them. After 1815, however, the fear of foreign
competition abated: it was no longer a shortage, but a
surplus, of labour, skilled and unskilled alike, that
seemed to legislators to constitute the danger. And so,
in 1824, the laws prohibiting the emigration of workmen
(and the export of machinery) were repealed, and
British labour, like British capital, was free to move to
any country willing to receive it.

It would be wrong to leave the impression that the
growth of the manufacturing population was entirely,
or even mainly, the result of increased geographical
mobility. There is, indeed, no evidence of any mass
exodus from the English countryside to the industrial
towns, and it seems likely that the redistribution of
labour took place largely in less abrupt ways. Little by
little men and women who had previously divided their
activities between agriculture and weaving or mining
came to work full-time at the loom or the coal face,
without moving their households. The tradition that
sons and daughters should follow the occupations of their
parents was weakening, and so it was possible for factory
employment to expand by drawing in more children,
and for domestic employment to contract as the number
of young entrants fell short of that of the adults who died
or retired. But, without proper statistics, it is impossible
to say how much weight should be attached to each of
these tendencies.

What is certain is that by 1830 Britain had, in one way

or another, obtained a body of wage-paid worker acclimatized to factory conditions and able to mo from place to place, and from employment to emplo ment, as occasion required. Rates of pay had come respond more quickly to local changes of demand ar supply, and to vary with the upward and downwar swings of general activity. Wages in one industry we linked with those in another, and, in particular, t earnings of farm labourers and builders moved up an down with those of the factory operatives. Instead of number of local and imperfect markets in which me offered their services to a few employers on whose goo will they depended for work, there was coming int being a single, increasingly sensitive, market for labou

CHAPTER V

'INDIVIDUALISM' AND 'LAISSER-FAIRE'

IN the eighteenth century the characteristic instrument of social purpose was not the individual or the State, but the club. Men grew up in an environment of institutions which ranged from the cock-and-hen club of the tavern to the literary group of the coffee-house, from the 'box' of the village inn to the Stock Exchange and Lloyd's, from the Hell Fire Club of the blasphemers to the Holy Club of the Wesleys, and from the local association for the prosecution of felons to the national Society for the Reformation of the Manners among the Lower Orders and the Society of Universal Good Will. Every interest, tradition, or aspiration found expression in corporate form. The idea that, somehow or other, men had become self-centred, avaricious, and anti-social is the strangest of all the legends by which the story of the industrial revolution has been obscured.

It would have been remarkable indeed if, in a community so compact of associations, the industrialist had remained aloof from his fellows. The hedges that were rising about the fields, and the factory walls that enclosed the workers and machines, were not the symbols of a growing individualism but the conditions of a more efficient administration of resources. The firm itself was less often a one-man concern than a partnership each member of which brought to a common stock his special gift of skill, capital or knowledge of the market. The partners of one firm were in close, and often daily, contact with those of other firms. They met as worshippers at the same church or chapel, as privates or officers in the same company of Volunteers, as members of the same club of anglers, or as riders or spectators at the same local meet. Many were subscribers to one or other of the bodies which sought to extend to the provinces the activities of the Society of Arts or the Smeatonian Club of London, and in this way they shared (though no doubt to a limited degree) their knowledge of improvements in technique. It is not to be supposed that their corporate endeavours were always, or even generally, directed to beneficent ends. For, as Adam Smith remarked, 'people of the same trade seldom meet together, even for merriment or diversion, but the conversation ends in a conspiracy against the public, or in some contrivance to raise prices'. Many an innocent-looking social or scientific group was, it seems likely, a business organization, the real purpose of which was to blunt the edge of competition and regulate output, prices, wages or the terms of credit, in some particular trade.

It was in the mining and metal-producing industries that combination reached its greatest height. The coalowners of the Tyne had for long contrived to keep up the price of fuel in London by limiting the 'vend' and assigning quotas to individual collieries. When the mines of the Wear, and later those of the Tees, were opened up, their proprietors were drawn into the organization; and, with short interludes of open trade, regulation continued till—long after the end of our period—the railways came to the rescue of the consumer with supplies of coal from inland fields. The smaller productive units in metal

ining had less economic power. In the middle years
of the eighteenth century the copper-miners of Cornwall
were, indeed, themselves exploited by the smelters of
Bristol and Swansea, who had associated to press down
the price of ore. When, however, in the 'eighties,
Thomas Williams began to develop the rich resources of
Parys Mountain in Anglesey, the situation of the Cornish-
men became so acute that (with the support of Boulton,
Watt, Wedgwood, and Wilkinson) they formed a defen-
sive alliance. Like most cartels, the Cornish Metal
Company fixed prices at such a high level that output increased and sales declined; and, in spite of an agreement
with the Anglesey partners for a division of the market,
the accumulation of stocks became so great that, in 1792,
the organization broke down. But for the war, which
brought large orders from the Admiralty, both Cornwall
and Anglesey might have presented, at this early stage,
the spectacle of the depressed area with its surplus
capacity, unemployed labour, and falling standards of
life.

In the iron industry the raw material came from so
many scattered sources that it was hardly possible for
those who mined it to control the market. But from the
early years of the eighteenth century the owners of
furnaces in Lancashire and South Wales had been in the
habit of fixing the prices both of the charcoal they
bought and the pig iron they sold. As the process of
smelting with coke developed, the Darbys and the
Wilkinsons entered into agreements as to the charges
they should make for steam-engine parts; and, before
1777, the ironmasters of the Midlands were holding
regular meetings to determine the prices of pig and bar
iron and castings. In 1799, on the initiative of Joseph

Dawson of Low Moor, the smelters and founders
Yorkshire and Derbyshire set up a similar organization
and, within a short time, there had come into being ye
other associations in Scotland and South Wales. Durin
the first decade of the new century these district societic
sent delegates to quarterly meetings, representative of th
industry as a whole, and until well into the 'thirtie
regulation continued on both a regional and a nationa
scale.

At the same time the users, no less than the producer
of copper, iron and other metals were drawing mor
closely together. The silver-plate manufacturers c
Sheffield, the steel manufacturers of Birmingham, th
file-makers of Warrington and Liverpool, the nailsmith
of Staffordshire, and the pin-makers of Bristol, Glou
cester and other places, each had their own organizatior
There was, indeed, hardly a single branch of the semi
domestic, metal-working trades that was untouched b
the tendency to combine.

In industries where the number of firms was large, th
variety of products wide, and markets scattered, th
exercise of control was less easy. The records of th
pottery trade provide instances of agreed price-lists fo
years as far apart as 1770, 1796, and 1814, and those c
the cotton industry give evidence that spinners i
Lancashire were accustomed to exchange information o
prices with others in Scotland. It was, however, to th
breaking down, rather than the setting up, of exclusiv
privilege, that the efforts of the potters and cotton-me
were turned. Led by Wedgwood, the first managed t
nullify the monopoly of china clay that had been grante
to William Cookworthy and Richard Champion; and
under the guidance of Peel, the second succeeded i

obtaining the revocation of the patents of Arkwright. In 1784 both groups joined hands with the ironmasters and the manufacturers of Birmingham to protest against a proposed excise on fustians, coal, and transport. And when, in the following year, Pitt announced his intention of admitting Ireland to the colonial and foreign trade of Britain, they organized the opposition and took the lead in founding a General Chamber of Manufacturers, with Wedgwood as its chairman.

This ambitious project to enable the industrialists to exert pressure on 'the great council of the nation' was destined, however, to reveal cleavages rather than to demonstrate unity. In 1786–7, when Eden was framing his commercial treaty with France, a difference arose between the delegates of the older trades of London and those of the newer industries of the provinces. The manufacturers of silk, ribbons, paper, glass, and leather had experienced no revolution in technique : their chief markets were at home, and their fears were of competition from the foreigner. The men of cotton, iron, brass, and earthenware, on the other hand, were eagerly reaching out to the newly discovered powers of steam : they had little cause for anxiety about imports from France, and their products were already finding outlets abroad. After the signing of the Treaty the debates in the Chamber became so acrimonious as to lead Boulton, Garbett, Wilkinson, and Wedgwood himself to withdraw, and it was then only a matter of time for the organization itself to dissolve.

The plan to set up a federation of British industries was at least a century in advance of the age. After the disappearance of the Chamber the manufacturers made few attempts to intervene in affairs. In 1796, and again in 1806, the ironmasters were successful in opposing th project to put duties on coal and iron. Commercia societies, which sprang up at Manchester, Leeds Birmingham, Glasgow and other places, made frequen representations on the obstacles that war and policy put in the way of trade. At a later stage the Chambers o Commerce that grew out of these were to play a signifi cant part in the repeal of the Corn Laws and the institu tion of Free Trade. But in general the instinct of the industrialist was to eschew politics. It was not by the arts of lobbying or propaganda, but by unremitting attention to their own concerns and their specialized trade organizations, that, after the end of our period they became a power—perhaps the greatest power—in the State.

The corporate sense of labour, like that of capital found expression in many forms. The situation of the domestic workers, scattered as these were, was hardly such as to make combination easy. Yet even in the first half of the eighteenth century there was a vigorous growth of clubs among the wool-combers, weavers tailors, nail-makers and other craftsmen. Most of these hid their true purposes under titles which implied the activities of friendly societies, and in many respects they were nearer to the gild of early times than to the trade union of to-day. In trades where almost every adult had his assistant or apprentice the line between employer and workman was not easily drawn. In Lancashire many small employers subscribed to the box, and in Sheffield both masters and men met at an annual candle-light supper, or took wine together at the *King and Miller* on Saturday nights. In the West Country, however, the planes of cleavage were more sharply defined, and here the course of industrial relations was broken by frequent strikes. But in each of the textile and metal areas the points at issue were much the same. Union activities were directed to the regulation of entries to the trade, to the suppression of 'unfair' workers, and to appeals to authority to give effect to the Elizabethan Acts relating to wages.

As time went on the language of organized labour began to take on a more strident note, and from 1760 the coalfields, the ports, and the textile villages were often scenes of violence. In 1765, the pitmen of the Tyne, on strike against the introduction of a leaving certificate, cut the winding ropes, smashed the engines, and set fire to the coal underground. In the later 'sixties jenny riots in Lancashire led to the destruction of machines and houses—and, perhaps, to the flight of Hargreaves and Arkwright to Nottingham. In 1773 the sailors of Liverpool staged a pitched battle in which (as Mr. Wadsworth tells us) they hoisted the 'bloody flag', sacked the houses of the shipowners, and trained cannon on the Exchange. Not all such disturbances, however, are to be taken as evidence of the existence of unions. Some were merely a spontaneous reaction to hunger or oppression, and the organization behind them collapsed as soon as the battle had been lost or won. But in the skilled trades, and among the millwrights in particular, the unions seem to have had a more or less continuous life. Towards the end of the century there was a lusty growth of friendly societies, and it is not without significance that many of these had an occupational basis and that it was in the growing centres of factory production—in Lancashire, Yorkshire and Lanarkshire—that the development was most marked. The women and children employed in the frame-spinning mills were, it is true, too weak to combine. But in the 'nineties the men who worked the jennies in the factories, the mule-spinners, and even the hand-loom weavers, had built up strong organizations. Already the sense of a common interest was leading local bodies to federate, and in times of strife men in one industry were beginning to give aid to those in another. By the end of the century trade unionism was no longer a matter of sporadic and temporary association: it was beginning to appear as a movement.

More than 200 years earlier, the State had made provision for the regulation of labour, and, though the statutes were now rarely enforced, it was held that to seek to increase wages, other than by appeal to the Justices, was illegal or even a crime. So long as a union remained passive it was left undisturbed, but the outbreak of a dispute was often the occasion for the employers to petition for an Act to put down combination in the trade concerned. Before the end of the century the number of such pieces of legislation (not all of which, however, were enforced) exceeded forty; and in 1799 the master millwrights of London, at odds with their men, were seeking yet another Act of this kind. Britain was at war: the ruling classes feared that unions might serve as a cloak for corresponding societies or other, more revolutionary, bodies. When, therefore, Wilberforce proposed that the millwrights' Bill should be extended to cover workers in all occupations, opposition was small. The Act of 1799 laid down that any person who joined with another to obtain an increase of wages or a reduction of hours might be brought before a magistrate and on conviction, sentenced to three months in prison

When it was realized that the magistrate might be an employer, and even a party to the dispute, there were loud protests; and, as a result of these, the measure was superseded by another, not very different in substance, in the following year.

The Combination Act of 1800 has been given unwarranted prominence in the histories of trade unionism in Britain. As Mrs. Dorothy George has shown, it was in fact rarely invoked—partly, no doubt, because the penalties it imposed were relatively light. In most instances where workers were indicted for combining (as in the famous case of the compositors of *The Times* in 1810) the action was one for conspiracy under the Common Law, or for breach of some measure relating to a particular trade. The whole apparatus of penal legislation was, indeed, of less effect than might have been imagined. Many unions were formed in the first quarter of the nineteenth century, and some of these operated in the open, without any action being taken to put them down.

The law of combination applied to employers no less than to workers. No one who has looked at the correspondence of industrial concerns of the period can have any doubt that the masters were often guilty of infringing it. Yet there were few, if any, prosecutions for conspiracy to force down wages. The difference of attitude in the two cases could not fail to impress itself on fair-minded men, and especially on those who were imbued with the doctrines of Adam Smith and Jeremy Bentham. Francis Place (1771–1854), the tailor of Charing Cross, who had himself suffered in early life from the austerity of the law, took up the cause of the trade unions. Aided by Joseph Hume, he succeeded, in 1824, in obtaining the removal

of the disabilities of the workers under the Common an
Statute law of combination. Immediately large number
of unions that had lived underground came into the open
New societies were formed, and, since 1824 was a year
prosperity and mounting prices, many claims were pu
forward for advances in wages. All this led to secon
thoughts on the part of the politicians. A Bill wa
brought in, and passed in 1825, which, though it con
firmed the legality of combination, imposed penalties o
workers who might be found guilty of molesting
obstructing or intimidating others. It was left to th
Courts to determine, over long years to come, what wa
meant by each of these ambiguous terms.

The four or five years of falling prices that followed th
collapse of the boom of 1825 were unfavourable to trad
union activity, and most of the strikes of this perio
failed in their objects. In the early 'thirties, under th
leadership of John Doherty and Robert Owen, scheme
were advanced for the amalgamation of societies and th
formation of a single Grand National Consolidate
Trades Union. The idea was as premature as that of th
industrialists, half a century before, for a Genera
Chamber of Manufacturers. It was not by a sudde
creation of this kind, but by a painful process of layin
brick upon brick, that the national unions, as we kno
them to-day, were built up.

Not all the 'industrious poor' were able to organiz
their own defences. There were many who, because
low earnings, unemployment, disease or misfortun
were forced to rely upon charity. If the period gave ris
to much that was ugly and squalid it also threw up me
and women, such as Jonas Hanway, Elizabeth Fry, an

William Wilberforce, narrow, it may be, in creed, but wide in compassion. Most of the industrialists were too much wrapped up in their own adventures to be active in social reform. But there were some, like Richard Reynolds of Coalbrookdale, who were renowned for philanthropy; and the letters of others give evidence of more altruism than the text-books would have us believe. Nor were the politicians altogether insensitive to social abuses. The governments that passed measures 'for preventing the excessive use of spirituous liquors', for regulating the employment of poor apprentices, for abolishing serfdom in the coalfields of Scotland, and for suppressing the slave trade, were not just the instruments of a class devoid of humanity.

Generally, however, alleviation was the business, less of the individual or the State, than of the voluntary organization. Public relief was supplemented by bodies like the Society for Bettering the Condition of the Poor, the Marine Society, which provided for friendless boys' and the Philanthropic Society, which cared for deserted children and vagrants. One kind of distress was met by the Royal Humane Society ('for the recovery of persons existing in a state of suspended animation'). Another was the concern of the Society for Improving the Condition of the Infant Chimney-Sweepers. Yet another was the responsibility of the Society for the Relief of persons imprisoned for small Sums. Education was the province of the Society for the Propagation of Christian Knowledge, of the charity schools, and, later, of the Lancastrian and National organizations. And what is sometimes described as 'the' social evil was the special field of the Society for enforcing His Majesty's Proclamation against Vice. Some of these bodies confined their

K

activities to the Metropolis, but there were others tha
grew up in the provinces to deal with the problems o
industry and the new town: the Manchester Board o
Health, in particular, was a pioneer of sanitary an
factory reform.

If it cannot be held that the period of the industri
revolution was one of individualism—at least in th
narrow sense of the term—it may with some justice b
maintained that it was an age of *laisser-faire*. This unhapp
phrase has been used as a missile in so many politic
controversies that it now appears battered and shabb
But there was a time when it was employed, not as a
epithet of abuse, but as an inscription on the banners o
progress.

The belief that the Tudors and Stuarts had a co
sistent plan for the conduct of economic relations di
hard. The regulation of wages, employment, technic
training, industrial location, prices, and commer
established by them was, in fact, less generous, le
enlightened, and less systematic than is sometimes su
posed. However that may be, the diminution of th
powers of the Crown and the weakening of the Priv
Council in the seventeenth century meant that some a
least of the instruments of control were allowed to ru
At the same time the rise of wider markets, more elabo
ate techniques, and more specialized types of labou
must have made the task of detailed supervision difficu
indeed. Even if there had been no Civil War, n
Glorious Revolution, and no rise of new classes t
political power, central direction must almost certair
have broken down. For more than a hundred yea
before the industrial revolution the State was in retre
from the economic field.

There were points, indeed, at which it still clung to the [lin]es of its earlier front. There were still authoritative [cor]porations—trading concerns like the East India Com[pa]ny, and regulative bodies like the Cutlers' Company [of Hall]amshire—that owed a continuance of their powers [to] a grant from the Crown. And the whole field of [for]eign commerce, navigation, and imperial economic [rel]ations was subject to state interference. A series [of] economic writers and publicists had attacked the [ou]tworks of the system. In 1776 Adam Smith turned his [ba]tteries on a crumbling structure, and through his in[flu]ence on Pitt and, later, on Huskisson and others, [so]me breaches were made in the ramparts. *The Wealth [of] Nations* gave matchless expression to the thoughts that [ha]d been raised in men's minds by the march of events. [It] gave logic and system to these. In place of the dictates [of] the State, it set, as the guiding principle, the spon[tan]eous choices and actions of ordinary men. The idea [tha]t individuals, each following his own interest, [cre]ated laws as impersonal, or at least as anonymous, as [tho]se of the natural sciences was arresting. And the belief [tha]t these must be socially beneficial quickened the spirit o[f op]timism that was a feature of the revolution in industry. [E]xperience has taught us, however, that an industrial [soc]iety needs a framework of public services if it is to [op]erate without social discomfort. Some of Adam [Sm]ith's followers, intoxicated by the new doctrine, were [dis]posed to confine the role of the State to defence and [the] preservation of order : *laisser-faire* was extended from [the] economy to society at large. The extremists were [str]engthened by the teaching of Thomas Malthus, whose [Es]*say on Population* appeared when the industrial revolu[tio]n was in full stream; and here again the disciples

failed to observe the qualifications that the master h
made. If people always tended to grow in numbers
the means of subsistence increased there could never
a raising of standards for the mass of mankind:
give charity was only to pour oil on the flames. T
pessimism of Malthus, no less than the optimism
Smith, may have directed many to the comfortal
position of leaving everything alone. But fortunat
most Englishmen have too much good sense to walk
the light of abstractions, and the actions of men, as t
chapter has shown, were often better than their cree
or their theories.

With the best will in the world, the transition fr
farms and cottages to factories and cities could nev
have been smooth. If the legislative machine had turn
out statutes with the same speed as the mules turned o
yarn there would still have been social disorder. F
much of the overcrowding and squalor was the resu
of the fact that progress in science was then, as to-da
more rapid than that in administration. 'The remo
influence of arrangements has been somewhat neglecte
wrote Dr. Kay in 1832, adding to this meiosis that t
neglect arose 'not from the want of humanity, but fr
the pressure of occupation and the deficiency of tim
Experience under the Factory Acts of 1802, 1819, a
1831 proved that until a body of inspectors had be
trained it was little use laying down minimum conditic
of hours and work. The experience of boards of heal
showed that until there was a larger supply of medi
men and other professional experts not very much cou
be done to improve conditions in the towns. Colquho
and others might inveigh against the multiplicity
officials, but the Civil Service was, by modern standar

icroscopic, and local services hardly existed at all.
ot until the whole apparatus of government had been
rastically reformed and a body of qualified public
rvants had been called into being could life in urban
reas be other than squalid. If the individual revolution
as not able to bring its rewards in full measure to the
rdinary man and woman it is to the defects of adminis-
ative, and not of economic processes, that the failure
ust be ascribed.

CHAPTER VI

THE COURSE OF ECONOMIC CHANGE

THE industrial revolution is to be thought of as a mov
ment, not as a period of time. Whether it presents its
in England after 1760, in the United States and German
after 1870, or in Canada and Russia in our own da
its character and effects are fundamentally the sam
Everywhere it is associated with a growth of populatio
with the application of science to industry, and with
more intensive and extensive use of capital. Everywhe
there is a conversion of rural into urban communities an
a rise of new social classes. But in each case the course
the movement has been affected by circumstances
time and place. Many of the social discomforts that ha
been attributed to the industrial revolution in Brita
were, in fact, the result of forces which (for all we kno
would still have operated if manufacture had remain
undeveloped and there had been no change of econom
form.

Among these was the movement of prices. In the fi
half of the eighteenth century wholesale prices in En
land were steady, with a slight inclination to fa
Between the middle 'fifties and the early 'nineties th
rose by some 30 per cent., and between 1790 and 18
they roughly doubled. From this point there was a fa
swift at first, then more gradual, until in 1830 a lev
was reached slightly below that of 1790, and less th
half that of 1814. For some of these fluctuations respo
sibility must, indeed, rest with the industrial revoluti

or it was of the essence of this that resources should be turned from the making of consumers' goods to that of industrial equipment, and the transfer could hardly have taken place without some alteration of values. After 1760 a larger proportion of the labour force of Britain came to be employed in constructing roads, canals, harbours, ships, factories, and machines, and a smaller proportion in producing food and drink, boots and clothes, furniture and houses. It might be thought that, in due course, the new instruments would have led to a greater output of finished commodities, and that the prices of these would have fallen. But economic processes were frustrated by political adventures; and it was not until the last fifteen years of our period that the industrial revolution could yield its harvest in the form of a more abundant supply of goods for the ordinary consumer.

Although throughout the eighteenth century the volume of silver coin turned out by the Mint was small, that of gold was growing, and the total amount of metallic money almost certainly increased. Banks and business men, moreover, were active in creating a currency of notes and bills: after 1797, this rose to large, and indeed to inflationary, proportions, and prices were forced up. From 1815, however, the Government and the Bank began to reduce the circulation; during the depression of 1816–17 many country banks were forced to close their doors, and there was a sharp drop in the level of prices. In the 'twenties the import of precious metals from South American mines failed to keep pace with European needs; and the conditions under which the gold standard was established in 1821 called for a continued contraction of paper. At a time when the output of goods was increasing, the supply of mone remained constant or declined, and in these circun stances prices could hardly do other than fall.

Rising prices are frequently associated with expansio and falling prices with contraction, of activity. It woul be wrong, however, to think of the period from 1760 t 1814 as one of unbroken prosperity, or of that fro 1815 to 1830 as one of continuous depression: each wa marked by ups and downs, some at least of which, again proceeded from causes independent of technological o industrial change.

For centuries economic life had been dominated by th yield of the soil, and even after Britain had becom largely industrialized the state of the crops was a matte of perennial anxiety. Throughout the first half of th eighteenth century the harvests had generally bee good, but there had been times when (as in 1709-10 1727-8, and 1739-40) adverse weather for two season in succession had brought a sharp upward movement o the price of bread. Since the greater part of the expendi ture of the poor was on food, a bad harvest was neces sarily followed by distress. That it must also have bee followed by industrial depression is not, at first sight clear; yet many contemporary observers—from the Lancashire rhymester Tim Bobbin, to the Scottis economist Adam Smith—assert quite plainly that dear ness of food led to falling wages and lack of work. It i obvious that when ordinary people were forced to spend more on bread they would have less left over to buy clothes and other commodities. But it is no less obvious that the farmers and landlords would find their incomes correspondingly enlarged. It would not be unreasonable to hold that increased expenditure by these would offset

creased expenditure by the rest of the community, and
that the state of industrial activity should, therefore, have
remained unchanged. Apart, however, from the fact
that the relatively well-to-do landlords and cultivators
would not want the same goods as the poor, it is doubtful
whether very much of their fortuitous profit would be
spent at all. Evidence from many different times and
places suggests that as income increases the proportion
that is hoarded tends to rise. And if this is true of mankind in general it is especially true of the man of the soil;
or, as William Cobbett (who knew him) said, the
farmer's maxim 'is to keep the money that he takes as
long as he can'. It was because the purchasing power
that came to the cultivator trickled so slowly through his
closed fingers that periods of poor harvests (such as
1756–7, 1767–8, 1772–5, 1782–3, 1795–6, 1799–1801,
1804–5, 1809–13, and 1816–19) were usually followed by
stagnation of trade, falling wages, and unemployment.

Government policy was directed to keeping agricultural prices at a level high enough to make farming
profitable. By a series of measures the growers of grain
were protected against competition from overseas; and
under the Corn Bounty Act of 1689 (which remained in
force until 1814) there was a subsidy of 5s. on each
quarter of wheat exported, so long as the price at home
did not exceed 48s. It is true that in years of dearth
exports were generally prohibited, and imports allowed
a duty free. But, though such expedients did something
to relieve hunger, they could not prevent a bad harvest
from having at least some adverse effects upon industry.
For the decline in the value of exports, and the increase
in the value of imports, often led to a fall in the rate of
exchange, and hence to a contraction of credit and

depression of trade. No fiscal device, however ingeniou
could eliminate the effects of the harvests. It was n
until Britain had become a creditor nation, with ove
seas assets to absorb the shock, that a deficiency in tl
current balance of payments could be looked on witho
grave concern.

According to Mr. Fussell, during the eighteenth ce
tury the area of land under wheat was enlarged by abo
a third, and the yield per acre raised by about a tent
But the growth of population was such that, after tl
middle of the 1770s, Britain ceased to be an export
and became, in most years, an importer of grain. N
was it only for cereals that she was coming to rely on tl
foreigner. Many other articles of diet, like tea ar
sugar, were brought from abroad, as well as such ra
materials as cotton, flax, wool, silk, and timber. F
markets also, especially those of the textile and hardwa.
trades, the people of Britain now looked overseas. Fro.
1760 to 1785 there had been a moderate expansion in tl
annual volume of exports; but as the industrial revol
tion gathered momentum, sales to foreign countries, ar
especially to those of Europe, increased in spectacul:
fashion. If imports of grain did something to allay or
source of instability, this growing reliance on inte
national trade brought with it another; and, from tl
middle of the 'eighties, the earnings and employment
a far larger number of English workers than ever befo
came to depend on what was happening abroad. Tl
prosperity of 1792, 1799-1801, 1809-10, 1815, an
1824-5, was largely connected with a rise, and tl
depression of 1793, 1811, 1816, 1819, and 1826 with
fall, of export demand. Sometimes the turn from boo
to slump was sudden; and the close connexions

London houses with financial institutions abroad meant that an adverse wind, blowing from Europe or America, not infrequently precipitated a crisis.

At the same time pulsations of investment at home gave rise to fluctuations of employment. When money was cheap and hopes of profit ran high, enterprising men set labour to work in creating industrial plant or building up stocks of materials; and since those engaged in these tasks had larger incomes to spend, firms that made goods for consumers shared in the prosperity. After a time, however, the increased demand for funds forced up rates of interest: expectations of profits fell, and the process of investment was checked. It is not to be supposed that a rise in the market rate of interest reacted at once on the ordinary manufacturing concern. As we have seen, the typical cotton-spinner or ironmaster was largely self-financing: he put back into his business all he could spare, without taking much thought of immediate returns. But to agriculture, building, and works of construction, a change in the price of money was of vital importance. Since bricks were used extensively, not only in the erection of houses and factories, but also in the sinking of mines and the making of canals and bridges, the variations of the numbers produced give an indication of changes of activity over a wide field. As Mr. Shannon has shown, the output of bricks rose and fell (about a year later) as the rate of interest moved down or up. And since higher or lower earnings in one part of the economy led to corresponding movements elsewhere, conditions of well-being, or those of adversity, became general. When a period of activity in construction coincided with good harvests and large exports (as in 1792, 1810, and 1815) there was high prosperity, and when none of these conditions existed depression was deep.

The oscillations of employment were often caused, and still more often magnified, by political forces: over much of the period of the industrial revolution Britain was at war. In some important respects, the men of the eighteenth century were more civilized than those of to-day: a state of hostilities did not put an end to intercourse between individual Britons and Frenchmen; and, since governments had not yet learnt how to control the lives of their subjects, warfare was never what we now call total. The losses of men and ships were serious indeed, but, these apart, physical destruction was small. It was through the distortion of the economic system, and the disturbance of social relations, that the most serious loss was sustained.

The war of 1756-63 resulted in a rise of prices and interest, a fall of real wages, and an over-stimulation of shipbuilding and the manufacture of iron. It was the seed, moreover, of the dispute with the colonies, which had adverse effects on commerce, and which led to the disaster of 1775. The eight years that followed the outbreak of war with the Americans brought a serious fall of both imports and exports—the only long-sustained decline of the century. They were marked also by a rise in the rate of interest, and by a decrease of investment at home: it was not until 1792, on the eve of a yet greater conflict, that the yield on Consols was back at the level of 1775. In the years of peace of the late 'eighties, however, there was much activity in building and public works; and 1792 presented all the symptoms of a boom. Early in the following year the demand for workers was such that farmers in various parts of the country asked Parliament

to prohibit the employment of labourers in cutting canals
during the months of harvest; and, in the light of what
we now know of the trade cycle, it is clear that a recession
was near.

The outbreak of hostilities with France in this year
was the occasion of a crisis the essential feature of which
(as of all financial crises) was an acute shortage of cash.
Fearing for the future, men hoarded their money; merchants were unable to obtain remittances from abroad,
or to continue credits to their clients at home; there was
a run on the banks, and many houses that were far from
insolvent went down for want of coin and notes. The
situation was met by a loan from the Government to
merchants, in the form of Exchequer bills, and within a
short space of time normal dealings were restored. Very
soon, however, it was the turn of the Government to be
embarrassed by lack of resources. Loans were raised
from the public and the proceeds spent, to a large extent
overseas. The cost of maintaining the armed forces
abroad, and the need to make a loan to the Austrian
ally, led to a fall in the rate of exchange. After the dis-
astrous experiment with the *assignats*, France had
restored a gold standard, and balances that had been
held for safety in London were now being repatriated.
So great was the drain of coin and bullion that in 1797
it was necessary to relieve the Bank of England of the
obligation of meeting its notes in gold. After the suspen-
sion of cash payments there was no compulsion on either
the Bank itself or the country banks to exercise restraint
in the discounting of bills, and so, in time, the volume
of the currency expanded, and the level of prices was
raised. By 1810 it was plain that sterling had fallen in
value in terms not only of goods, but also of foreign

currencies and gold. There was much debate then, and there has been more since, as to whether the responsibility for the inflation lay with the Bank of England or the private banks. In fact, it lay with the Government, which by borrowing, and spending the proceeds, raised the money income of the public out of all proportion to the volume of goods available for civilian consumption. Some measure of inflation, it is now generally recognized, is necessary to the conduct of war. If statesmen had followed the advice of Francis Horner and his colleagues of the Bullion Committee of 1810, and had returned to gold at this time, there would have been a fall of prices so great as to put many people out of work and endanger the prosecution of the war. As it was, the rise of prices increased profits, and, since wages limped slowly behind the cost of living, the standard of life of the workers was lowered.

Government borrowing had another, no less important, effect. In 1792, when Britain was at peace, the yield on Consols had been 3·3: five years later it had reached 5·9. Many projects set on foot when money could be obtained at, or near, the first of these rates could not be continued when the cost of borrowing was raised. Capital was deflected from private to public uses, and some of the developments of the industrial revolution were once more brought to a halt. Expenditure on men-of-war, munitions, and uniforms gave a stimulus to shipbuilding, the manufacture of iron, copper and chemicals, and to some branches of the woollen industry. But the progress of the cotton, hardware, pottery, and other trades suffered a check. In the first phase of the war, building was greatly curtailed, but the peace of 1801–3 brought a revival, and between

304 and 1815 construction (though not that of houses)
was maintained at a fairly high level.

Foreign trade also suffered less than in earlier wars.
After a fall in 1793, exports mounted, with little setback,
to a peacetime boom in 1802. The renewal of hostilities
was marked by a decline; but for six years the volume
of trade was not unsatisfactory, and in 1809-10 there
was, once more, a boom. The attempt of Napoleon to
bring Britain to her knees by cutting off her markets was
a failure. Direct exports to western Europe, indeed, fell
away. But the islands of Heligoland and Malta became
spearheads by which British trade penetrated to the
heart of the Continent, and there was a growth of exports
to the West Indies, the United States, and South
America. When in 1810, however, Austria was forced to
make peace, and Holland was annexed by the French,
some of the channels of commerce were closed; and
when, in the following year, the Non-Intercourse Act
put a stop to trade with the United States, the volume of
British exports fell sharply. But the entry of Russia to
the conflict in 1812 brought Napoleon's Continental
System to an end; and, in spite of the naval war with
America, overseas trade remained good in 1813 and
1814 and rose to a peak at the end of the struggle.

Britain had for long offered warehousing facilities for
goods in transit from one country to another. During
the war it became a major aim of policy to deflect the
merchandise of the French West Indies, in particular, to
London, and then to re-ship it to Europe and elsewhere.
In 1790 about 26 per cent. of Britain's exports consisted
of goods of foreign origin: by 1800 the percentage was
44, and in 1814 it was still as high as 36. It would be
wrong, therefore, to infer that a high level of gross

exports meant that all was well with the industries th
looked for their markets abroad. The condition of t
cotton operatives and nail-makers, in particular, flu
tuated with each change in the fortunes of battle an
each shift in the tactics of statecraft. But, on the whol
Britain rode through the storm with her people at wor
the price of wars for the civilian is paid less when th
are in progress than when the fighting has ceased.

In April 1814 Napoleon surrendered his throne an
was banished to Elba. For several months British indu
try was borne on a rising wave of optimism: the rate
interest fell, there was a drop in the price of bread, an
both exports and production for home markets we
high. But before the end of 1815 the boom had broke
Demobilization threw some 300,000 men on the labo
market at a time when industry had not yet adjuste
itself to conditions of peace. (The records of the Po
Law are eloquent of the fate of many of these.) Eur
pean demand for British goods had fallen off, an
Government expenditure had been cut by a hal
Merchants and industrialists were oppressed by th
knowledge that, sooner or later, the monetary standar
was to be restored at a parity that could be maintaine
only if prices were lowered. Private investment was at a
ebb and unemployment was widespread. Poor harves
in 1816 and 1817 caused food prices to rise and th
demand for manufactured goods to fall. In 1818, indee
conditions improved. Low rates of interest, revived Gov
ernment expenditure, better harvests, livelier marke
abroad, and a raised level of construction at hom
brought a brief boom. But the three following year
were less favoured; and it was not until 1821 that th
era of inactive capital and unemployed labour—th

a of what we now call reconversion and deflation—was
rought to an end.

The experiences of these years have clouded for many
he true nature of the technical and economic changes
f the period. Just as the war had thwarted the purpose,
o the conditions in which peace was restored postponed
he fulfilment of the revolution in industry. There was,
here can be no doubt, alongside the distress, a growth
f class feeling and bitterness. Much of this arose, less
om a conflict between capital and labour, than from
n opposition of views as to where the burden of in-
reased taxation should lie. A Parliament representative
argely of landlords demanded the repeal of the income
ax, which had been imposed as a war measure, and the
ntroduction of increased duties on grain. It was sub-
mitted, not without reason, that the agricultural classes
lready bore, through the land tax, the tithes, and the
oor rates, the greater part of the cost of the public and
cclesiastical establishments. And it was urged, with
ess justice, that the political services which the land-
wners rendered entitled them to special consideration
om the State. The Corn Law of 1815, which prohibited
he release to the millers of wheat from abroad so long
s the price at home was below 80s. a quarter, was in-
ended to preserve for the agriculturists a structure of
rices and rents that had been created by war—at a
ime when manufacturers were being forced to sell their
roducts more cheaply, and when money wages tended
o fall. In fact, the domestic price of wheat rarely
eached 80s. The defect of the law was not that it
naintained a consistently high level of prices for grain,
ut that, in times of dearth, it prohibited relief from
broad until conditions approached those of famine.

L

Apart from this fiscal injustice, the workers ha
grounds for complaint. Some, instructed by Tom Pain
and William Cobbett, resented their lack of politica
status, and many had learnt by experience of the limit
the law of combination imposed on their bargainin
strength. Throughout the eighteenth century, riots ha
been endemic: again and again the pitmen and sailors
shipwrights and dockers, and the journeymen of th
varied trades of London downed tools, smashed windows
and burnt effigies of those with whom they were a
variance. About many such incidents there had bee
something of the light-heartedness of the May Da
demonstration. But the tumults of the second decade c
the nineteenth century sounded a deeper and more dis
turbing note. Those who took part in them were not, i
the main, factory operatives, but workers who belonge
to the older system of industry: the croppers of Yorkshire
the frame-work knitters of Nottingham, and the hand
loom weavers of Lancashire. Under-employed and
under-fed men were not over-nice in theorizing as to th
cause of their distress, and it was natural enough tha
they should strike at the machines that appeared to b
taking the bread from their mouths. Some of the unem
ployment was, indeed, the result of technical change
but the chronology of revolt points to the real cause o
the trouble. It was in 1811, and again in 1816, whe
political events and bad harvests had led to depression
that the Luddites destroyed the stocking-frames in th
Midlands and the power-looms in the North. It was i
1817 that the hungry and workless Blanketeers set off o
their dismal march from Ardwick Green. And it was i
1819, when, once again, bread was scarce and trade a
low ebb, that the working-class Reformers of Lancashir

athered, and suffered, at St. Peter's Field. The story of
ppression—of the Home Office spies and the infamous
ix Acts—has been told too often to bear repetition here.
rightened politicians and an inept administration were
ot the least of the misfortunes of these unhappy years.

In the early 'twenties many circumstances combined to
roduce high prosperity. The currency was established
n a foundation of gold and there was a run of favourable
arvests. Huskisson and his colleagues were active in
pulling down tariffs, lowering excise duties, and removing
estrictions from industry and trade: the policy of reform
y repeal was good in the eyes of men who had been
ked by controls and who asked only to be let alone. A
ubstantial part of the National Debt was converted from
to 4 or 3½ per cent.: in 1820 the yield on Consols had
een 4·4; by 1824 it was 3·3. In 1822 Bank rate, which
ad stood for almost half a century at 5, was brought
own to 4. But Bank rate was not yet a mirror of
market conditions, and in the early months of 1825
hort-term loans were being placed at little more than
½ per cent. In Lancashire and Scotland factories were
un up at unprecedented speed, and between 1821 and
825 the output of bricks more than doubled. Ironworks
vere busy producing piping for gas and water under-
akings and sections for bridges and railways. Stocks of
:otton, wool, and other raw materials were built up.
Overseas trade expanded; and, since re-exports now
:onstituted only 16 or 17 per cent. of the goods sent
abroad, the growth was almost entirely the outcome of
ncreased productivity of industry. Canning's recogni-
ion of the emancipated colonies of Spain, in 1823, gave
a fillip to foreign investment: Latin America seemed to
offer boundless opportunities for trade, and the export

of capital to this area played a large part in th
boom.

High expectations of profit led to a burst of speculativ
schemes in 1825: many of these were bogus, and other
inherently sound, failed to yield returns as fully, or a
promptly, as had been hoped. Since incomes and price
had risen, the exchanges took a downward turn, an
there was an almost simultaneous internal and externa
drain of gold. Correctives were applied. Interest rate
were raised and credit was contracted: prices fell an
unemployment became widespread. It is unnecessary t
detail the story of the depression of 1826, the recovery o
1827, the prosperity of 1828, and the gloom and agricul
tural distress of 1829 and 1830. The cyclones an
anti-cyclones of the 'twenties were of the same natur
as those that were to pass over England many time
in the later decades of the nineteenth century.

It was through such changing seas that the captain
of the industrial revolution steered their courses. Man
of the difficulties they encountered were, it is clear, of thei
own making. Some of the navigators were unable t
distinguish a false wind from a true, and not all kne
when it was safe to clap on sail, or prudent to shorten it
Not all, again, took sufficient thought of the state of thei
crews: pioneers have often suffered disaster by reason o
this. But the major troubles arose, not from wan
of skill or want of heart—certainly not from want o
courage—but from the forces of Nature and the current
of political change. If harvests had been uniforml
good; if statesmen had directed their attention to pro
viding a stable standard of value and a proper mediun
of exchange; if there had been no wars to force up

prices, raise rates of interest, and turn resources to destruction, the course of the industrial revolution would have been smoother, and its consequences would not have been, as they are, in dispute.

Some of these consequences, it must be admitted, were baleful. In spite of the efforts of Thomas Percival and James Watt, the skies over Manchester and Birmingham grew dark with smoke, and life in the cities became drab. The smaller industrial town, like Oldham or Bilston, had a harsh countenance: towns, to be good, should grow slowly. There was, it seems likely, a decline of taste—as the very letterpress of the books to which the student goes for his data bears witness. But all was not loss. The face of England is patient of modulation: enclosing landlords and planters gave it new grace. Nor were the early industrialists insensitive to the appeal of the country: the beauty of Cromford and Millers Dale suffered little by the enterprise of Arkwright, and stretches of the Goyt and the Bollin owe something to Oldknow and the Gregs. Even the products of manufacture are not to be thought of as wholly uncomely: Telford's Anglesey bridge and the pottery of Wedgwood and Spode cry out against that. If large-scale industry overshadowed art and craftsmanship, it did not by any means destroy them.

Much has been written about the effects of the industrial revolution on the workers. Some, impressed by the lot of those who went down in the struggle against the machine, have declared that technological change brought little but misery and poverty, and a statistician of repute has set on record his opinion that by the early years of the nineteenth century the standard of life of the British worker had been forced down to Asiatic levels.

Mr. Colin Clark can hardly have looked at the statisti
which more than a generation of research has produce
The careful studies of Mrs. Gilboy indicate that, over tl
eighteenth century, the material well-being of tl
labourers in the woollen area of the South-West ha
indeed, fallen, but that the lot of his fellow in the texti
region of the North had steadily improved, and that tl
labourer of London more than held his own. It is tr
that the rise of prices after 1793 made many humb
people poorer. But before the end of the war (as Profess
Silberling has shown) industrial wages in Englar
caught up with retail prices, and in the 'twenties tl
gain was pronounced. In 1831 the cost of living w
11 per cent. higher than in 1790, but over this span
time urban wages had increased, it appears, by no le
than 43 per cent.

It would have been strange, indeed, if the industri
revolution had simply made the rich richer and the po
poorer. For the commodities to which it gave rise we
not, in general, luxuries, but necessaries and capit
goods. The tardiness with which the last of these yielde
their fruit to the consumer has already been explaine
But by the 'twenties the effects of the war were passir
away and the cottons and woollens, and food and drin
which now became available, were consumed not by tl
few, but by the masses. Some of the products of tl
factories and ironworks were sent abroad, but the retur
cargoes did not consist, in the main, of wines and silk
but of sugar, grain, coffee, and tea for the people
large. Much has been made of the suggestion that tl
prices of the things Britain exported fell more rapid
than those of the things she brought back: there was r
revolution to reduce costs in overseas agriculture; ar

British lending abroad may also have helped to give the terms of trade an unfavourable turn. But, though such influences may explain why, in the 'thirties and 'forties, real wages were lower than might have been expected, they had little effect, it would seem, between 1815 and 1830. The diet of the worker almost certainly improved: there was a substitution of 'flower of wheat' for rye and oatmeal; and meat, which had been a rarity, became, with potatoes, the staple dish on the artisan's table. Not all the coal raised from the pits went to feed the furnaces and steam-engines: a warm hearth and a hot meal were of no small consequence to the man who came home wet from the fields.

In 1802 George Chalmers remarked that the laborious classes were 'too wealthy to covet the pittance of the soldier, or too independent to court the dangers of the sailor'. There were, true enough, many vagrants and paupers, but, even before the new Poor Law came in, the hordes of the 'indigent and distressed' had probably shrunk. Hours of labour were long, and holidays few; there is a mass of evidence that employment in factories was harmful to the health and morals of the young. A leading politician has recently spoken of the 'mechanized horrors of the industrial revolution', and there can be little doubt that the deeper mines and more complicated machines brought new risks of mutilation and death. But against all this must be set the lessening of strain on those who worked in the heavy trades, and the decline in the number of crippled and deformed people that followed the introduction of power in places like Sheffield. There must be set, also, the reduction of sweating of women and young children, the rise in family earnings, the greater regularity of pay, and the gain in welfare that came as industrial work was taken out of the home

Whether the houses themselves were becomin better or worse is difficult to determine: much depend on the periods compared. Many of the dwellings pro vided for the workers by the country factory master have survived—at Cromford, Mellor, and Styal. The have design and proportion, and, even by moder standards, are not wanting in amenity and comfort. Bu these were put up when building materials were plen tiful, wages relatively low, and money relatively cheap After 1793 the import of timber from the Baltic wa restricted, and the price of labour of bricklayers and carpenters went up. At least two-thirds of the rent of a dwelling consists of interest charges: rates of interes were rising, and for more than a generation they re mained high. This meant that if dwellings were to b let at rents which the workers could afford to pay the had to be smaller and less durable than those of th 'eighties. The rows of ill-built, back-to-back houses, int which the rapidly growing population of the towns wa pressed, were largely the product of wartime conditions

After 1815 matters were made worse by the influx o Irish, who, gregarious by instinct, crowded into the sea ports and the towns of the North. Careful estimates mad by members of the Manchester Statistical Society in th middle 'thirties led to the conclusion that about one sixth of the families in Manchester were Irish, and tha the percentage of the people living in cellars was 11·75 In Liverpool, where again there were many Irish, n less than 15 per cent. of the inhabitants were in cellars But in the newer towns, which were the special creatio of the industrial revolution, conditions were far less grim In Bury, where there were few Irish (and few hand-loom

weavers) only 3·75 per cent., and in Ashton-under-Lyne
only 1·25 per cent., of the people were housed in this
way. In these places, the investigators reported, the
houses of the workers were not only less crowded, but also
better furnished and cleaner than those of the cities.

An historian has written of 'the disasters of the industrial revolution'. If by this he means that the years
1760–1830 were darkened by wars and made cheerless
by dearth, no objection can be made to the phrase. But
if he means that the technical and economic changes
were themselves the source of calamity the opinion is
surely perverse. The central problem of the age was
how to feed and clothe and employ generations of
children outnumbering by far those of any earlier time.
Ireland was faced by the same problem. Failing to solve
it, she lost in the 'forties about a fifth of her people by
emigration or starvation and disease. If England had
remained a nation of cultivators and craftsmen, she could
hardly have escaped the same fate, and, at best, the
weight of a growing population must have pressed down
the spring of her spirit. She was delivered, not by her
rulers, but by those who, seeking no doubt their own narrow ends, had the wit and resource to devise new instruments of production and new methods of administering
industry. There are to-day on the plains of India and
China men and women, plague-ridden and hungry,
living lives little better, to outward appearance, than
those of the cattle that toil with them by day and share
their places of sleep by night. Such Asiatic standards,
and such unmechanized horrors, are the lot of those who
increase their numbers without passing through an
industrial revolution.

BIBLIOGRAPHY

THE standard work on the subject is P. Mantoux, *T Industrial Revolution in the Eighteenth Century* (1928). E cellent introductions, written from different points view, are contained in A. Redford, *The Economic Histo of England, 1760–1860* (1936) and in J. L. and Barbar Hammond, *The Rise of Modern Industry* (fifth ed., 1937 The student should also consult C. R. Fay, *Great Britai from Adam Smith to the Present Day* (1928), A. P. Usher, *History of Mechanical Inventions* (1929), W. Bowden *Industrial Society in England towards the End of the Eighteen Century* (1925), and, for the later phases of the movemen J. H. Clapham, *An Economic History of Modern Britai* Vol. I (1926). Much of the best and most recent wor however, is to be found, not in books, but in articles, to numerous for special mention here, in the *Econom History Review*, *Economic History* (annual supplements t the *Economic Journal*), and the American *Journal Economic History*.

Some will find it best to approach the subject throug the study of a particular region, such as is offered b A. H. Dodd, *The Industrial Revolution in North Wale* (1933), H. Hamilton, *The Industrial Revolution in Scotlan* (1932), J. D. Chambers, *Nottinghamshire in the Eighteent Century* (1932), and W. H. B. Court, *The Rise of the Mi land Industries, 1600–1838* (1938). Others who wish t concentrate on the story of a particular industry hav the range of choice presented by Lord Ernle, *Englis Farming, Past and Present* (new ed., 1936), Naomi Riches *The Agricultural Revolution in Norfolk* (1937); H. Heaton *The Yorkshire Woollen and Worsted Industries from th Earliest Times up to the Industrial Revolution* (1920), E Lipson, *History of the Woollen and Worsted Industries* (1921) W. B. Crump, *The Leeds Woollen Industry, 1780–182* (1931); A. P. Wadsworth and Julia de L. Mann, *Th*

Cotton Trade and Industrial Lancashire, 1600–1780 (1931);
G. W. Daniels, *The Early English Cotton Industry* (1920);
T. S. Ashton, *Iron and Steel in the Industrial Revolution*
(1924); T. S. Ashton and J. Sykes, *The Coal Industry of
the Eighteenth Century* (1929); and H. Hamilton, *The
English Copper and Brass Industries to 1800* (1926). More
specialized studies of industrialists include Samuel
Smiles, *The Lives of the Engineers* (1861–2), G. Unwin,
A. Hulme, and G. Taylor, *Samuel Oldknow and the
Arkwrights* (1924), H. W. Dickinson and Rhys Jenkins,
James Watt and the Steam Engine (1927), T. H. Marshall,
James Watt, 1736–1819 (1925), H. W. Dickinson, *Matthew
Boulton* (1937), E. Roll, *An Early Experiment in Industrial
Organization* (1930) and T. S. Ashton, *An Eighteenth-
century Industrialist: Peter Stubs of Warrington, 1756–1806*
(1939). Among biographies of leading men of the
period, G. D. H. Cole, *Life of William Cobbett* (1924),
and the same author's *Robert Owen* (1925) are of special
value.

Books on population and social conditions include
A. M. Carr-Saunders, *The Population Problem* (1922),
G. Talbot Griffith, *Population Problems of the Age of
Malthus* (1926), M. C. Buer, *Health, Wealth and Population
in the Early Days of the Industrial Revolution* (1926), M.
Dorothy George, *London Life in the XVIII Century*
(1925), A. Redford, *Labour Migration in England, 1800–
1850* (1926), and Ivy Pinchbeck, *Women Workers in the
Industrial Revolution, 1650–1850* (1930). The standard
work on combinations of labour is Sidney and Beatrice
Webb, *History of Trade Unionism* (new ed., 1911); and a
vivid account of the lives and aspirations of the workers
is given by J. L. and Barbara Hammond in *The Village
Labourer* (1911), *The Town Labourer* (1917), and *The
Skilled Labourer* (1919).

For the political, religious, and social theories of the
period the student is advised to go direct to the works

of contemporary writers, but he will find help in Bas
Willey, *The Eighteenth-century Background* (1940), G. E
Bryson, *Man and Society: The Scottish Inquiry of th
Eighteenth Century* (1945), F. A. Hayek, *Individualism, Tr
and False* (1946), E. Lipson, *A Planned Economy or Fre
Enterprise* (1944), Isabel Grubb, *Quakerism and Industr
before 1800* (1930), and W. J. Warner, *The Wesleya
Movement in the Industrial Revolution* (1930). For a detaile
account of the Dissenting Academies he should see H
McLachlan, *English Education under the Test Acts* (1931)

Among works on finance and commerical policy ar
A. E. Feavearyear, *The Pound Sterling* (1931), Sir Joh
Clapham, *The Bank of England* (1944), Henry Thornton
Paper Credit of Great Britain (1802 ed. F. A. Hayek
1939), A. Redford, *Manchester Merchants and Foreig
Trade, 1794–1858* (1934), and C. R. Fay, *The Corn Law
and Social England* (1932). Statistical information on
prices is to be obtained from N. J. Silberling, 'British
Prices and Business Cycles, 1779–1850' (*Rev. of Economi
Statistics*, prelim. Vol. V, Supplement 2); on wages,
from Elizabeth W. Gilboy, *Wages in Eighteenth Century
England* (1934), and G. H. Wood, 'The Course o
Average Wages between 1790 and 1860' (*Economic
Journal*, 1899); and on rates of interest from G. F
Warren and F. G. Pearson, *Gold and Prices* (1935).

For other statistical information the student should
consult earlier authorities, such as G. Chalmers, *Estimate
of the Comparative Strength of Great Britain* (1802) and P.
Colquhoun, *The Wealth, Power and Resources of the British
Empire* (1815).

H. A. Shannon's valuable article on 'Bricks: A Trade
Index, 1785–1849' is printed in *Economica*, 1934, and the
student will find a very useful summary of the fluctua-
tions of economic activity in W. Rostow, 'Business
Cycles, Harvests and Politics' (*Journal of Economic
History, 1946*).

INDEX

ADEMIES, 20
riculture, 7, 23–8, 59–64;
oard of, 13, 62
prenticeship, 3, 53, 111–15
kwright, Richard, 17, 34,
1–2, 90, 94, 102, 105, 131
ts, Society of, 13, 21, 62,
28
nospheric engine, 37

KEWELL, ROBERT, 62
nks, 100–7, 149–50
ls of exchange, 101, 103,
06
ding of labour, 53, 111–12,
18–19
ck, Joseph, 16, 20, 67, 78
aching and dyeing, 76–7
ulton, Matthew, 21, 68, 105,
29, 131
cks, 147, 155
dgewater, Duke of, 17, 82–4,
05, 122
ndley, James, 14, 82–4, 120

LICO PRINTING, 76
nals, 81–4
pital, 7–11, 84, 94–109;
xport of, 108, 156; import
of, 107
rron Ironworks, 65, 68, 90
rtwright, Edmund, 13, 17,
74
amber of Manufacturers,
31
emicals, 76–9
ild labour, 55, 113–16, 119
ubs, 127, 132
albrookdale, 40, 65, 68, 90

Coal-mining, 34–9, 64–5
Cobbett, William, 22, 145, 154
Coke of Holkham, 16, 27, 62
Combination Act, 135
Combinations of capital, 128–
32
Consols, 9
Corn Laws, 145, 153
Cort, Henry, 14, 65–6, 121
Cotton industry, 31–4, 70–5,
112–18
Crises, 104
Cromford, 72, 90, 157, 160
Crompton, Samuel, 13, 14, 18,
73
Crowley, Ambrose, 17, 43, 53
Currency, 99, 143–4, 149–50
Cutlery trade, 42–3

DALTON, JOHN, 16, 20–1
Darby, Abraham, 40–1, 98
Davy, Humphry, 13, 16, 65
Dawson, Joseph, 17, 18, 130
Debt, 50, 55
Domestic system, 49–56, 71
Dundonald, Earl of, 20, 78,
112, 118

EMBEZZLEMENT, 54, 109
Emigration, 3–4, 124–5
Enclosure, 23–6, 59–61
Engineering, 37, 81–8
Etruria, 80–1, 90, 122
Exports, 146, 151

FACTORIES, 33, 73–4, 112–18
Factory Acts, 115, 140
Fluctuations of trade, 144–56
Fly-shuttle, 33

Frame-rents, 32, 55
Friendly societies, 107, 132, 133

GARBETT, SAMUEL, 77, 131
Gibbon, Edward, 5
Gott, Benjamin, 21, 75, 97, 109
Greg, Samuel, 113, 116, 157

HAND-LOOM WEAVERS, 117
Hargreaves, James, 71
Harvests, 144–6
Hat manufacture, 32
Hosiery trade, 32
Hours of labour, 122–3
Houses, 160
Huntsman, Benjamin, 42
Hutton, James, 16, 78

INTEREST, RATE OF, 9–11, 24, 58, 82, 83, 91–2, 99, 107, 108, 117, 147, 148, 150, 152, 155, 160
Invention, 13–15, 88–9
Investment, 9–10, 107–8, 147
Irish immigration, 3, 117, 124, 160
Iron industry, 39–41, 65–7

JENNY, 14, 71
Johnson, Dr., 11

KAY, JOHN, 33
Keir, James, 16, 17, 77
Kennedy, John, 19, 116
Knight, Edward, & Co., 10

LABOUR, 50–6, 109–26
Laisser-faire, 138–41
Lombe, Thomas, 13, 33
London, 49
Long-pay, 52–3, 99, 118
Lovell, Lord, 16, 27
Lunar Society, 21

MACADAM, JOHN, 19, 78–9,
M'Connel, James, 19, 116
Malthus, Thomas, 6, 20, 13
Manufacturers, Chamber 131
Maudslay, Henry, 88, 90
Metcalf, John, 85
Migration, 61, 124
Mobility, of capital, 9, 106 of labour, 50, 110, 123–
Monopoly, 12
Mule, 13, 14, 73, 116
Murdoch, William, 14, 110, 122
Mushet, David, 19, 66

NAIL INDUSTRY, 42–3
National Debt, 8, 108, 155
Neilson, J. B., 19, 67
Newcomen, Thomas, 18,
Newton, Isaac, 15
Nonconformity, 18
Norfolk system, 27–8

OLDKNOW, SAMUEL, 98, 1 157
Open fields, 23–4
Owen, Robert, 113, 136

PATENTS, 12, 90
Paul, Lewis, 33
Peel, Robert, 94, 100, 113– 115, 130
Percival, Thomas, 21, 115,
Place, Francis, 135
Poor Law, 110, 112, 117
Population, 3–6, 48, 161
Ports, 44
Potatoes, 7, 159
Pottery industry, 79–81, 1 130
Power loom, 74–5, 117
Prices, 142–3, 149

stley, Joseph, 16, 20, 21, 3

ters-out, 31, 32, 52

AKERS, 18, 42, 43, 87

LWAYS, 86–7
nolds, Richard, 86, 90, 37; William, 16, 90
s, 154
ers, 45–6
ds, 44, 84–6
buck, John, 17, 18, 20, 21, 5, 68, 77
er-spinning, 14, 33
ation of crops, 28, 60

ETY LAMPS, 13, 65
ery, Thomas, 37
ings, 7–8; banks, 107
lement Laws, 110, 123
manufacture, 30, 33
clair, Sir John, 19, 62, 118
eaton, John, 86
th, Adam, 12, 78, 128, 35, 139, 144
o works, 68, 88, 90
enhamland, 110–11
ndard of life, 63–4, 150, 57–9
am engine, 68–70
el, 41–2
el-mill, 36
ohenson, George, 13, 65, 7
ck Exchange, 106–7
bs, Peter, 17, 95, 109

Styal, 113, 160
Symington, William, 86

TELFORD, THOMAS, 19, 85
Tennant, Charles, 77
Terms of trade, 159
Textiles, 28–34, 70–6
Townshend, Viscount, 28
Trade, 46–7
Trade unions, 132–6
Trevithick, Richard, 87
Truck, 54, 100
Tull, Jethro, 27
Turnips, 7, 27, 28
Turnpikes, 44, 85

UNIVERSITIES, 19–20, 67
Usury Laws, 9

WAGES, 126
Walker, Samuel, 17, 95–7, 102
Wars, 8, 148–52
Watt, James, 12, 16, 18, 19, 20, 21, 67–70, 77, 86, 110, 129
Wealth of Nations, 22, 139
Wedgwood, Josiah, 13, 16, 21, 80, 97, 121, 125, 129, 130, 131
Wesley, John, 18, 22
Wilberforce, William, 134, 137
Wilkinson, John, 21, 65, 68, 70, 100, 102, 129, 131
Women workers, 29, 30, 32, 35, 51, 118, 119, 120
Woollen industry, 28–30, 75–6

YOUNG, ARTHUR, 62

Printed in Great Britain by
The Camelot Press Ltd., London and Southampton